THOMAS MULLER
The Story of a True Champion

A special thank you to Yonatan Ginsberg, Yaron Ginsberg, and
Guy Ginsberg.

Editor: Y. Ginsberg

Design: Lazar Kackarovski

Cover picture: AP Photo/Matthias Schrader

Library of Congress Cataloging-in-Publication data available.

ISBN: 978-1-938591-43-3
E-ISBN: 978-1-938591-47-1

Printed in the United States of America.

www.solebooks.com

To my three grandfathers:
Henry Kunstmann, Franc Part, and Max Koren

Thomas Muller
The Story of a True Champion

Michael Part

Sole BOOKS

More in the Soccer Stars Series:

The Flea – The Amazing Story of Leo Messi

Cristiano Ronaldo - The Rise of a Winner

Neymar The Wizard

Harry Kane - The Hurricane

James – The Incredible Number 10

Antoine Griezmann – The Kid Who Never Gave Up

Eden Hazard – The Wonder Boy

Balotelli – The Untold Story

Luis Suarez – A Striker's Story

www.solebooks.com

CHAPTER 1
SECOND PLACE

The microphones were in place on stage and hundreds of reporters and fans lined the walkways and the catwalks of the World of Sports at the Adidas headquarters in Herzogenaurach, Germany. The CEO of Adidas picked up one of the microphones and looked at someone in the shadows, just offstage, and gave him a nod.

Thomas Muller, hidden in the shadows, nodded back and waited for his cue.

The fans on the walkway watched the festivities below, and a three-story picture of Thomas adorned the empty space that separated the floors of the modern building. There were two words on the picture: *Servus Thomas*. It meant, *Hi Thomas!*

The awards presentation was solemn, but Thomas had a hard time staying serious himself. These days, he was so happy, everything made him laugh, and that made him feel like doing funny things. Besides soccer and his wife, one of his favorite things in life was making people laugh. It had always been this way, ever since he used to crack-up his older cousins and younger brother Simon when they were little kids. FIFA was going to interview him after they handed him the trophies. He already knew what he was going to say. He wished his younger brother Simon could have been there. He could not get time off work. The two of them had shared everything growing up, and he wanted to share these awards with him as well. For that matter, he wished all his soccer mates from his hometown team, TSV Pähl, could have been there.

It had been a long trip from the High Castle and roadways of Pähl to world champion.

As the people on stage spoke enthusiastically about the 2014 World Cup with Germany triumphant for the first time in twenty-four years, Thomas stared at the larger-than-life picture of himself hugging his teammate Mats Hummels and other friends from his youth. The picture had been taken on the pitch at the famous Maracanã stadium in Rio, seconds after they had won their final match against Argentina and clinched the 2014 World Cup title. His mouth was wide open and his tongue was out, like he was at the dentist getting a filling.

A man in a suit wearing headphones tapped his shoulder. "Ready?"

Thomas turned to him and made the same wide-mouthed expression.

The guy laughed.

Thomas laughed with him. Then he took a breath. Making someone laugh always relaxed him.

"Ladies and gentlemen," the man on the stage said, and everyone grew quiet. "Please give a warm welcome to our World Cup champion, Thomas Muller!"

The crowd erupted in applause.

Thomas trotted out onto the stage. He'd loved the stage ever since he had acted in a schoolplay in elementary school. The first time he'd stepped onto the stage as a young boy had felt great, and it felt amazing now. The excitement and the jubilation, knowing that so many eyes were staring at him, expecting him to entertain them. It was the same excitement he felt whenever the ball he shot toward the goal darted inside the net, a second before the roar of the crowd exploded.

On that October evening, every person in Germany was in love with the humble boy from the Bavarian countryside town of Pähl.

"Thank you," he said, and the crowd cheered. He turned and smiled. That was when he noticed the head of Adidas wasn't holding the Silver Boot trophy for second-highest scorer in the World Cup. He was only holding the Silver Ball award. Where was the other trophy he was supposed to receive?

"We have a surprise for you, Thomas," the man said and turned in the other direction, looking just offstage. "Come on out!" he shouted.

The nearby elevator doors opened and there was his younger brother, Simon, standing there, holding the Silver Boot trophy. He hurried over to them.

Thomas smiled and fought back the tears. He had not seen Simon in months and missed him terribly. He grabbed him and gave him a powerful bear hug that almost made him drop the trophy. He nodded at the trophy and whispered in his brother's ear, "Is that for me?"

Simon grinned. "I hope so, it's got your name on it!" he whispered back and the two laughed.

Simon handed him the Adidas Silver Boot trophy.

The audience applauded and cheered wildly from all directions.

Thomas held the trophies tight to his chest. Second-best player and second-highest scorer. Nice, he thought, but more importantly, he was a player on the number one team in the world.

After the ceremony, Thomas made sure Simon stood next to him. He did not want to let him out of his sight while he was interviewed for FIFA. "Thomas, you've just received your individual awards for your performances at the World Cup. How important are they to you?" the reporter asked.

Thomas grinned. "They are an acknowledgment of what I have achieved. But... this is success at an individual level. They are important, but winning the World Cup is everything. Not only for me or for my team, but for Germany."

"What, for you, was the most crucial factor in winning the title?" the reporter asked.

Thomas laughed. "Winning!"

The audience went crazy and cheered some more.

He felt the love from his fans, and he hoped they felt it from him because he spoke from the heart.

It had to be about winning, he thought. Scoring goals and winning. Every coach he had ever played for had drilled that into him. It was the first trophy his country had won since Oliver Bierhoff played for the national team and scored the golden goal that won the Euros in 1996. He'd been just a little kid playing for his hometown team in Pähl when Germany won the Euros. Germany had not won anything since.

Until now.

And now they were world champions.

He turned and smiled at his younger brother, who was taller than him, and remembered how they had come to this point.

All the way from their grandmother's farm in Unterdorf in Pähl, Bavaria, and later, when he was four years old, nearby Oberdorf, where he'd lived surrounded by beautiful lakes and forests, a real-life castle, and cows.

Even the cows had been beautiful, he thought.

It was a place where everyone knew your name.

Where everyone was friendly and supportive.

And where everyone was crazy about the beautiful game.

CHAPTER 2
THE GOLDEN TEAM

Five cows of various shades lined up along the wooden fence and watched as four-year-old Thomas Muller kicked the ball down the road. When he passed them, all their heads moved in unison from left to right, like they were watching a tennis match. At least, that was what it looked like to *him*.

His cousins – Andreas, who was seven years older; Matthias, who was two years older and called Thias; and Johannes, who was three years older – leaned against the fence, a few posts down from the cows, watching with great interest as their younger cousin kept the ball close to his foot and flicked it from one side of the road to the other, never faltering, never making a mistake, and never losing it in the grass beside the road. They were all taller than Thomas, but not by much.

"Nice one!" Thias shouted.

"Where'd you learn how to play like that?" Andreas shouted.

"From you!" Thomas shouted back with a laugh, and all the boys joined in. He kept going until he got to the yellow sign announcing the village's name, *Pähl*. He picked up the ball and walked back. "What's up? What are you guys doing here?"

"What does it look like?" Andreas asked, snapping his fingers, asking for the ball with a flick of his right hand.

Thomas obeyed and tossed it to him.

"Pick-up," Andreas said. "Me and you against *these* two losers!"

"Hey! Who you calling a loser?!" Thias shouted back at him, pretending to be insulted. He grabbed the ball from Andreas, let it drop, and dribbled it away. Johannes raced after him, and the two of them flicked the ball back and forth to each other as they made their way up the street toward the village.

Thomas appeared out of nowhere and stole the ball. It was as if he knew where the ball would be, even before Thias kicked it to Johannes.

"Hey! Where'd *he* come from?!" Johannes said to Thias, surprised.

"I'm the invisible man!" Thomas said and ran back up the road toward Andreas.

"After him!" Thias shouted and charged after Thomas. When he caught him, he tried to steal the ball back. Instead, Thomas nutmegged him. In the confusion, Thias tripped over his own feet and cartwheeled into the grass on the side of the road.

Andreas laughed so loud, he almost fell over. Then he blocked Johannes, and the move allowed Thomas to run by.

Thomas had his eyes on the goal. It wasn't the garage doors at his grandmother's farm. It was a much more difficult shot – the V of a big tree where the trunk had split from being struck by lightning. The big one at the bend in the road. The magical one. He gave the ball a kick, and it sailed through the air, veered right into the V, and stuck there!

Thomas raised both his arms in the air. "GOOOAAAAALLLL!!!"

Thias and Johannes trotted back, chuckling at Thomas because no one else in the family or in the neighborhood was as into the game as him. Thias was covered in dust from his fall and as they walked quickly, he pulled handfuls of straw from where it had fallen down his pants.

"I'll get you for that, kid!" Thias shouted.

Thomas giggled.

"I think we taught him too well!" Andreas said, then turned to Thomas. "Training pitch at TSV Pähl is open, let's go play on a *real* field."

"With the team!?" Thomas asked.

"Who knows?" Andreas said. He turned away from Thomas and rolled his eyes, then walked up the street ahead of Thomas, shoulder-to-shoulder with Thias and Johannes.

"Here," Andreas said, tossing the ball over his shoulder without looking. "Have a party."

Thomas caught the ball on his chest and let it drop to the ground. His foot took over and dribbled it along. All he could see was a wall of guys with their backs to him. And all he could think about was how much they put him down for being younger. So, he shot the ball into the back of Andrea's head.

"Ow!" Andreas said. He spun around and glared at his cousin.

"Oops! Sorry, Andreas!" Thomas said. "I meant to hit Thias. Maybe when I get a little older."

"Okay," Andreas said. "Come!"

Thomas giggled and raced ahead, pulled alongside the older boys, and proudly marched with them. They turned around the next bend in the road that was close to an area thick with trees. Off in the distance were the Bavarian Alps.

Minutes later, the boys heard the shouting and the whistleblowing, the sounds of a match, and ran the rest of the way to TSV Pähl's club pitch.

Thomas loved going to the pitch. He had watched matches from the other side of the fence many times. Sometimes, his mother and father actually bought tickets, and they were able to sit in the stands. The grounds were behind a tall chain-link fence. The grass was dark green, cut short, and well-manicured. The lines and boxes were straight, and the goals were in perfect condition.

The long, tiled walkway to the white building that was the TSV Pähl sports hall was deserted, and they were able to walk right through to the field.

Right in front of the pitch was an old wooden shack with a big window in the front. It was all closed up. "Where's the guy?" Thomas asked. He meant the guy behind the big window who sold tickets. "Don't we gotta buy a ticket?"

"Not today," Andreas said, and the four boys entered the grounds.

There were two squads in the middle of a scrimmage on the field.

The F-Jugend squad of eight-year-olds were battling it out against their younger counterparts, all in yellow and black.

Andreas draped his arm over his cousin's shoulders. "What do you think?"

They all stood on the sideline at midfield and watched the practice match.

"They're all older than me," Thomas muttered. "A *lot* older."

Andreas grinned. "Me and Johannes and Thias are older than you, and you kick our butts every chance you get," he said. "Those G-kids are only three years older. I don't think they'd have a chance if you played against them."

Thomas flashed his cousin a grin. "Well, I *am* as tall as them."

"Exactly," Andreas said.

The ref blew the whistle, and the training stopped.

"C'mon," Andreas said. "I want you to meet someone." He guided Thomas out on the field toward the coach, Peter Hackl. He was medium height with dark hair and a full beard.

"He looks mean," Thomas said as they walked toward Hackl.

"No, he's nice, don't worry," Andreas replied. He was excited, and his voice trembled when he approached the coach.

"This is him," he said to Hackl. "Thomas Muller."

"Ah," the coach said.

Why is he so serious? Thomas thought.

"Thomas, this is coach Hackl," Andreas announced. "He has an idea he wants to talk to you about."

Peter Hackl put his hands on his hips and scowled at Thomas.

Thomas didn't know what to do, so he scowled back.

Hackl's expression softened, and he had to smile. "What year were you born?" he asked.

"1989," Thomas replied.

"Good." Hackl nodded, then turned to Andreas. "Let's see him in a scrimmage with the Gs first."

"Why?" Thomas asked. "They're too old for me."

"I'm going to make a team of boys like you, born in 1989." The coach started to walk away, then turned back with a smile. "Don't worry, Thomas. I know what I'm doing. Let's go."

"Now?"

Hackl turned back to him. "Yes, *now.*"

Thomas raced after him, and Hackl introduced him to the G-Squad at midfield.

"What do you play?" one of the boys asked.

Thomas shrugged. He was four years old, and no one had ever asked him that question before. "I'm a forward. But I can be a midfielder, or a defender, or even a goalkeeper."

"Anything else?" the kid asked. "How are you at ping pong?"

"Great!" Thomas replied. He wasn't sure why everyone laughed.

"Go up in the middle," Hackl said and nodded to the other boys, then walked away. As he left the field and blew his whistle, the scrimmage began.

At first, Thomas did not get the ball. He chased it like crazy, but the kids were really good. They were not only chasing the ball, they were passing.

But then an opportunity came. He stole the ball from a player in midfield and made a run into the box, sending the ball into the net, fooling the goalkeeper who dove into the opposite corner.

Hackl watched intently. He had seen many kids play, and he thought he had an eye for talent. *This kid*, he thought, *Thomas Muller, is special*. He was a natural, and he was fast. Hackl knew every kid who played soccer in the area, but they were all a bit older. He shook his head. Andreas had not exaggerated. The boy was good.

"What do you think?" Andreas asked.

"I want him," Hackl said. "He's gold. He'll go good with Seppi. They're the same age." Seppi was another talented kid who scored bundles.

"Great," Andreas said. "I'll let him know."

"No, I'll do it," Hackl said, putting his whistle in his mouth and ending the scrimmage.

All the boys charged over to him and surrounded him. Hackl smiled at Thomas. "I need to talk to your parents. If they agree, you are in."

The kids gave the younger player high fives. They knew he was good.

Josef Graf, who everyone called Seppi, turned to Thomas.

"I'm Seppi!" he said. "We're the same age." He stuck out his hand for Thomas to shake.

Thomas had seen his father do this, but no one had ever done it to him. He slowly offered his hand and the two boys shook.

"So, what do you have to say?" Andreas asked his cousin. "You're in!"

Thomas could not believe it. He hugged his cousin tightly.

"Hey, take it easy!" Andreas said, peeling Thomas off him.

"Where are you going?" he shouted a moment later.

Thomas was already running toward home. He wanted to break the news to his parents and his brother and his grandmother. His heart was filled with happiness. He had just been picked to play on a real team.

His cousins rushed after him, but Thomas was faster than them and he left them in the dust. In his head, he saw himself dressed in the team uniform, scoring one goal after another. But his greatest dream was when he saw himself raising his hands in the air and seeing his whole family in the stands, cheering. Even his grandfather was there. He'd loved soccer more than life. Thomas felt the same way.

CHAPTER 3

GRANDMA ERNA
HAD A FARM

The next week, at the Burkhart farm in Unterdorf Pähl, all forty cows stood together in the pouring rain, occasionally sticking out their tongues to catch the big warm raindrops and occasionally shaking the water drops off their backs. It made quite a racket.

Thomas had to stay inside, it was raining so hard. He sat glumly at the kitchen table, his soccer ball at his feet. He rolled it back and forth from one foot to the other, watching the rain pour down through the kitchen window.

Erna Burkhart, his grandmother, was at the stove wearing an apron she had made herself, cooking lunch. "Why the long face, my dear?" she asked while she fried up a cast-iron skillet full of *rissoles*, which were seasoned meatballs.

Thomas looked horrified and grabbed his face. "My face is long?!" he shrieked in terror. "Is it melting?!" He made a monster face, but he could not stay serious for long and finally broke down and laughed at his own joke.

Erna gave him a look. "It's an expression. You look sad."

"Oh," Thomas said, making his face normal again. "Whew. My face always gets long when I can't play cuz of the rain, Grandma."

Erna raised an eyebrow. "Play inside. No one who loves soccer likes the rain. Here, I made your favorite. Pork rissoles and potato salad." She slid a plate under his nose with one hand and dumped three rissoles and a scoop of potato salad onto it with the other, then turned back to the stove.

Thomas put his face over the plate and took a deep breath. He loved the smell.

"Thank you, Grandma," he said, shoveling in a mouthful.

Erna saw him and frowned. "Hey slow down. What's the rush?"

Thomas stopped for a second. "I got a big match in a couple minutes," he said.

Erna raised the other eyebrow. "A big match? Who are you playing with? The squirrels?"

"No, the mice," he joked. "I'm playing in the basement."

Erna burst out laughing. "There aren't any mice down there!" she said, then thought about it for a moment and suddenly looked worried. "Are there?"

He shrugged, finished his plate, and grinned. "No, just me."

Erna chuckled. "Well, it's been much too quiet around here, anyway." She looked at him and smiled. "I'm going to bring your folks some rissoles. Think they'll like them?"

"Yes! Your food is the best, Grandma!"

Erna grinned. She enjoyed these conversations, especially if she cooked something good. "It will be nice once your parents finish building the house. Then you can sleep in your own bed."

"But I like it here, Grandma," he replied.

Erna smiled to herself. "Me too, sweetie," she said, wrapping the rest of the food up and placing it in a small basket. "Your father says the house will be finished in the spring. So you have plenty of time to get sick of me."

Thomas smiled. He liked her jokes.

He wiped his mouth, raced out of the room, and headed down the basement steps, taking them two at a time.

"Don't break anything," his grandma called after him, but he was already gone.

He looked up at the doorway at the top of the wooden stairs. "Okay," he said, then returned his attention to the cement room. There was a furnace on one of the long sides and a line of dormer windows near the ceiling that opened outward on the other. His grandmother said that was so coal could be poured in and used to feed the furnace that kept the farmhouse warm in the winter. No one used coal anymore, so they were just windows.

The ends of the room had been cleared and marked as goals by two dust-covered stuffed chairs at each end.

Thomas dropped the ball to his feet and gave it a kick at the wall in front of him, right between the chairs.

THUMP!

Erna listened. And smiled.

THUMP!

There it was again.

Down in the basement, Thomas flicked the ball from one foot to the other as he weaved between imaginary players.

"Gooooaaaallll!" He spun around and flew backward into one of the stuffed chairs on either side of the goal, throwing up a cloud of dust.

Upstairs, Erna leaned against the wall by the front door. She loved that her grandson never held back. She was thrilled that he loved soccer more than the rest of them in the family, even more than her late husband, God rest his soul. She lingered a little longer and listened to Thomas playing in the basement below her feet, then realized they needed to get going and hurried to the door. Her son-in-law Gerhard and her daughter Klaudia would be hungry from all that heavy lifting of building a home.

"Okay, Thomas, the match is over!" she shouted. "Let's go."

The *Rainy Day Unterdorf Pähl Basement Cup* was over. Grandma Erna said so.

Outside, the asphalt was wet, but the rain had stopped. Erna carried an umbrella and hid under it out of habit. Thomas, wearing black rubber rain boots, made sure he splashed through every puddle along the way to *Oberdorf*, two blocks away. It was called *Oberdorf* because it was higher in altitude than Unterdorf; not by much, but enough to warrant a different name. The Muller's new home was small and practical, just like Thomas's father, who worked as an engineer at the

BMW motorcycle factory in Munich. The home was set back from the road with a fresh cement driveway, roped-off so no one could walk on it. Thomas's father's motorcycle was parked out front on the side of the road. Gerhard wore a yellow rain slicker covered in plaster and was on a low scaffold of metal and wood, spreading plaster on one of the outside walls with a silver trowel.

Thomas and his grandmother stopped in front. Thomas took out the soccer ref's whistle he carried with him in his pocket and blew it.

TWEEEEEEEEEEEEET!

The noise startled Gerhard Muller, and he slipped on the scaffold but grabbed the rail just before he fell.

"Papa! Lunch!" Thomas shouted.

Gerhard saw it was his son and mother-in-law and chuckled. He was tall and thin, with short-cropped light hair and blue eyes.

Thomas's mother, Klaudia, with bright blue eyes and dark hair cut short, came around the side of the half-built home pushing a baby buggy. She stopped when she saw her mother and her son and flashed a smile. "Excellent!" she said. "I'm famished!"

"Hey!" Gerhard laughed and leaped over the rail of the scaffold and landed on the ground. He trotted to his son and hugged him.

Thomas peeked into the baby buggy to see his little brother. He was just a year and a half old and looked cute. Thomas looked at his father and raised up his arms, and Gerhard lifted him up.

"How are you, son?" he asked.

"Great! I scored a lot of goals," Thomas replied.

"But it's been raining all day. Where did you play?"

"In the basement," Thomas said.

"By yourself?" His mother patted his head.

"Yes. And I won!" he said.

Everyone laughed.

Thomas grinned. There was only one thing as good as scoring a goal, and that was making everyone laugh.

CHAPTER 4
CHOCOLATE AND COMIC BOOKS

Thomas raced into Scholz's bakery and grocery store, holding his three-year-old brother's hand, and skidded to a stop at the comic book rack. Simon stopped when he stopped. Thomas started thumbing through the comics and Simon, much shorter, looked at the covers in the lower racks.

Norbert Scholz, the owner, watched bemused from behind the high counter. There was a pre-show for the World Cup quarter-final match playing on the radio behind the counter. "What are you doing here, Thomas? The World Cup starts in half an hour!"

"We'll make it, Mr. Scholz. I'm looking for something," Thomas said, never taking his eyes off the comics.

Simon tried to pull free, but Thomas did not let go.

Mr. Scholz jerked his thumb toward the radio. "Germany versus Bulgaria. It's going to be quite a match," he said.

Thomas looked up. "Yes sir," he said and went back to the comics.

"If you're looking for the new *Mickey Mouse*, we didn't get it in, sorry. How about a nice *Lucky Luke* or *Asterix*?" *Lucky Luke* was a comic about a cowboy and *Asterix* was a comic about a funny Gaul, which was the name of a French tribe in the year 50 B.C. Thomas liked them both, but if he had to choose just one, it would be *Mickey Mouse*.

Thomas smiled. "Maybe Mr. Scholz," he said. "Are you sure there aren't any *Mickey Mouses* in here?"

Norbert's wife, Rosemarie, came in from the back. "Of course, he is not sure," she said, flashing a new issue of the *Mickey Mouse* comic, waving it around proudly like a flag. "Because I have it right here."

Thomas's eyes lit up, and he raced to the front counter and reached up and took the *Mickey Mouse* comic from her hands like it was made of solid gold. "Thanks, Mrs. Scholz!"

"I put it aside for you as soon as it came in," she said to Thomas and gave her husband a sidelong glance. "Mr. Scholz only pays attention to the French and Belgian comics because those are the ones he reads."

"I don't read comic books," Norbert replied.

"Right," Rosemarie said. "Anyway, he doesn't pay attention to the American comics."

"That is not true, Rosey," Norbert said, scolding her. He leaned over the counter to talk to Thomas. "It's the quarter-final. Germany versus Bulgaria all the way from Giants Stadium in America. It starts soon," he warned. "You don't get to see *that* every day."

"Yes sir," Thomas said.

"Maybe we'll win. That would be something. Jurgen Klinsmann. He's a fantastic player!"

"I know," Thomas replied.

Rosemarie winked at Thomas. "Maybe someday you'll win it for us, eh? Maybe someday you will win it for Bayern, Thomas," she said. "I hear you are doing well over at TSV Pähl!"

Thomas's face turned beet red. "You do?"

"Yes, of course I do," she said.

The sounds of the crowd crackled and blared from the broken speaker on the radio.

Thomas stared at it. He imagined himself on the field. In his mind's eye, he watched where all the men were and then watched where they weren't. Just like he did in the street and on the pitch at TSV Pähl. It was the empty spaces – that was how you scored goals.

"What do you think, Simon?" Thomas asked. "Me and you at the World Cup someday?" Simon smiled up at his big brother. Thomas handed Rosemarie some chocolate he had chosen and the *Mickey Mouse* comic and paid for it all, and she put the candy in a bag and handed it all back to him.

"Maybe someday Mr. Scholz and I will come see a match of yours, Thomas Muller. We are still waiting for our invitations," Rosemarie said.

Thomas blushed. "Am I supposed to invite you?" He was mortified.

"I'm teasing," she replied. "But don't be surprised if you see us someday." She passed him a package of *Kaiser* rolls. "This is for your mother," she said. "It's her regular order, and she already paid for it, so take it straight back up the hill to that beautiful new home of yours. Talk about handy, your father! Building his own home." She let the thought drift off.

"Pre-game show, Thomas," Scholz warned. "Time to hustle! This is the knockout round!"

"Yes sir," Thomas said. He took the comic, candy, and *Kaiser* rolls in one hand and Simon in the other and raced out of the store, the bell jangling on the door as they went out.

It was just a few blocks' walk back to his new home. Thomas shared his chocolate with Simon along the way. They walked slow. Real slow. There were fields and pastures and cows along the way to distract them. By the time they reached the front door, the chocolate was all gone and the second half of the match had already begun. Gerhard sat on the couch staring at the screen, hypnotized, never looking at his sons. "Germany is up, one to zero," he said. "Where have you been? You knew the match was starting!"

"Sorry, Papa," Thomas said and plopped down beside him. Simon dropped beside him. "I was out at Scholz's getting some stuff."

Gerhard just nodded without taking his gaze from the screen. "Mathäus scored," he mumbled.

A half-hour later, in the 76th minute, Bulgaria's number eight, Hristo Stoichkov, nicknamed *El Pistolero*, the Gunslinger, knocked a rocket into the German net, equalizing the score.

Gerhard puffed out a frustrated sigh and leaned back on the couch. "What a player – he's playing for Barcelona's dream team!" he said. "They should have guarded him better!"

"It's a tie," Thomas said.

"Yes, but we can win, there is enough time," Gerhard said. As soon as he finished the sentence, he let a cry of despair, "Oh no!"

Bulgaria scored just three minutes after they tied.

"What?" Thomas jumped.

"They scored again," his father said. "I don't believe it."

"We are losing!" Thomas cried.

"No, we have still a lot of time," his dad said. He didn't want to show his desperation.

But when the ref whistled the end of the game, you could hear a sigh of despair bursting out from the entire country. No one had seen this coming.

"We can win the next game," Thomas said.

"There will be no next game for us," his father said. "We need to wait four more years for the next World Cup."

Gerhard was devastated. Thomas felt the tension and wanted to cheer his father up. He giggled and waved the *Mickey Mouse* comic book around like he was swatting flies. "I got a new *Mickey Mouse*!"

Gerhard tried to smile and reached out. Thomas handed the comic to him and he screwed up his face. "It's all sticky!"

"Oh, sorry, Papa. That's chocolate."

Gerhard looked at the sticky chocolate on his hand and frowned, then looked at his boys. Both of them had chocolate all over their faces.

He burst out laughing.

CHAPTER 5
SCHOOL DAYS

Thomas's mother laid out his school clothes for him before the sun came up. Pants. Underwear. T-shirt. Plaid shirt. Socks. Sneakers. Thomas watched her with one eye, pretending to be asleep. His mother wanted everything to be just right this day. It was 1996, and Thomas was starting elementary school. As soon as she was out of the room, he snatched up the plaid shirt, rushed over to his chest of drawers, yanked open the middle drawer, hurriedly pulled out his Bayern number 13 Muller jersey, threw the plaid shirt in, and closed the drawer.

His mother was at the kitchen table. Simon was next to her, spooning mouthfuls of *Weizen Gries* into his mouth. "You're gonna be late if you don't hurry!" she called to Thomas. "I should walk you to school, it's the first day!"

Thomas, wearing his Bayern jersey, was already sneaking by on his way out the front door. "Don't worry, mom, I'll be fine! Bye!" he called, then quickly ran out the front door.

Klaudia leaned against the kitchen cabinet and folded her arms. "Okay, if you say so," she said to herself.

It was just a short walk to his new school. Everything in Pähl was next to everything else; the church was next to the houses, the houses were next to the city hall, the city hall was next to the stores, the stores were next to the school, the school was next to the farm.

The farm behind the elementary school was more interesting to Thomas than the school building itself. It had a huge pile of dung and lots of geese flitting about, honking at each other. The school building was a brick two-story with a basement and dormer windows like the one at his grandma's farm.

Thomas knew about his new teacher because his cousins had told him about her. He saw her before he entered the classroom. She had medium-length hair and bright blue eyes. She wrote her name quickly on the blackboard.

His friend and teammate Seppi was already waving to him, so he sat behind him. "Morning!" Seppi whispered. "I was waiting for you!" Having a friend in his new class was a great relief to Thomas.

"Good morning, class. My name is Mrs. Hupfauf," the teacher said. She finished printing her name on the blackboard and jammed the stick of chalk into the board, making a messy period after her name. She waited. No one said a word. "This is where you say, 'Good morning, Mrs. Hupfauf,'" she said and turned and smiled at her new students.

"Good morning, Mrs. Hupfauf!" the class chanted in unison.

She picked up a short stack of thin books with brightly colored covers and waved them at the class. "These will be our reading books for the year," she said. "Besides the usual arithmetic and reading and social studies, we will also perform a play for the school. Some of you will even act in it. I know you find that hard to believe now, but you won't when the time comes. But that won't be until the end of the semester, so not to worry. Reading and writing and arithmetic first."

Thomas smiled. He was good in all those subjects. He already knew how to read, and he knew how to count and write on sheets of lined paper. He watched his teacher look around the room and thought she was cool so, when she looked at him, he gave her two thumbs up.

Mrs. Hupfauf stopped. She was not sure how to react. No one had ever given her two thumbs up before. "And you are?" she asked, scanning her roster.

"I am Thomas Muller, Mrs. Hupfauf!" he said, jumping out of his seat and standing at attention, flashing her a big smile. "Soccer legend."

She ran a bony finger down the roster, found his name, and checked it off. Then, she glanced up and saw what he was wearing and chuckled to herself. "So you are," she said.

He was standing there in his bright Bayern number 13 Gerd Muller jersey.

"Nice jersey," she said and continued writing on the blackboard. "Is Gerd Muller your favorite?"

"Not my *most* favorite, but Mario Basler is in the wash," Thomas replied.

She chuckled. "I knew your grandfather. He was a great soccer fan," she said. "Like you."

Wow, Thomas thought. Playing ball in the streets, he had learned from his cousins and the other older guys that it was not cool to like your teacher, but what was not to like? She was a soccer fan. And she knew his grandfather. He had died before Thomas was born, so he never knew him. But he'd heard tales about him, mostly from his grandma. When his grandfather was very old and weak and at the end of his life, he asked to be moved in front of the TV so he could watch the Bayern match. It was the last match he ever saw before he passed away, right in that chair. A game that Bayern won. Thomas's grandma had told him that story many times. In fact, practically everyone in Pähl knew the story. It was that kind of town, where everyone knew everybody else. And tales like that became legends.

Thomas felt the same way about Bayern Munich. It was his team, and he wore the jersey with pride. And he had a few of them: Basler, Mathäus, Scholl, and of course, Muller. He hated it when they got dirty because that meant he couldn't wear them, and he wanted to wear them every day. And he also bet his grandfather would have liked to see him wearing a Bayern jersey.

"You were all born in interesting times," Mrs. Hupfauf announced to the class. "Do you know why?"

"Because we are interesting?" Thomas replied and Seppi laughed out loud.

The whole class joined in, including Mrs. Hupfauf.

"Very funny, Thomas," she said.

Thomas blushed.

"Now I will ask *you* a question. Are we here to uncover how interesting you all are – and I am sure you are — or are we going to study, among other things, a little history?"

No one said a word. The room grew pin-drop quiet.

"You are all about the same age, which means you were all born in the same year, give or take a few months," she said and studied her notes. "For instance, you, Thomas. You were born on September 13th, 1989. Two months later, the Berlin Wall fell and Germany entered a new era. Can anyone tell me what happened the following year?"

Seppi's hand shot up.

Mrs. Hupfauf studied him for a moment. "Yes, Josef?"

"We won the World Cup. Germany against Argentina, one-zero."

Mrs. Hupfauf smiled. "Please let me correct you, Seppi. *West* Germany won. At that time, Germany was still a divided country. East Germany and West Germany. But on October 3rd of that same year, 1990, Germany reunified, and we became one again."

The bell rang. It was recess time. One of the kids took out a soccer ball from his backpack.

"Let's play!" he shouted and ran out with the ball. *Perfect*, Thomas thought. He and Seppi ran out to the schoolyard. He couldn't wait to have a game.

CHAPTER 6
THE BALL HOG

The field at TSV Pähl was misty the next training day, but Thomas didn't mind getting a little wet. He did not come to soccer practice to stay dry, or clean, or any of that stuff. He came to score goals and be with his soccer pals, especially Seppi.

The team was already on the field doing jumping jacks and Thomas hurried across the short-cropped grass and joined in.

Coach Hackl gave him the evil eye for being late. "Glad you could join us, Muller."

"Sorry coach, I…"

"That'll be an extra ten," Hackl said, interrupting him. "Dismissed," he said to the rest of the team then returned his attention to Thomas. "If you make it." He gave Thomas a wink to let him know it was serious, but not that serious, and jogged off. Thomas found himself on the mid-line doing jumping jacks in the wet turf all alone, watching his mates line up a short distance away. He rushed through the ten then sprinted to catch up to them, his squad of golden boys, who were all, according to his teacher, living in interesting times.

Hackl blew his whistle, and the boys scattered to do their warm-ups. Later, they passed the ball to each other in circles while a player in the middle tried to intercept the ball. They worked on their passing skills.

They practiced free kicks and corner kicks and building a proper wall, but what Thomas really looked forward to was the scrimmage that awaited them at the end of the practice. When the coach finally announced it was time, they split into two teams and played a short match. This was the time he felt the happiest.

Hackl thought it was fun to watch Thomas running down the field with the ball, outrunning everyone else on the team and scoring goals. He made it look easy. Thomas loved it every time he scored and waved his arms triumphantly.

Hackl watched, and it made him happy. He crossed his arms. When Thomas did it again, he raised an eyebrow. And when Thomas did it a third time, he blew his whistle and waved Thomas over.

He stood, arms crossed, as Thomas ran up to him. "You wanted me, Coach?"

"Take the bench, Muller," Hackl said.

Thomas's smile drooped into a frown. "But... What'd I do?" He felt like crying. He knew what he had done. He was hogging the ball. His cousins yelled at him for doing that sometimes when they played. It was really hard for him to share the ball. If no one could keep up and he had a chance to score a goal, was that so bad?

It was as if coach Hackl could read his thoughts. "Soccer is a team sport," he said. "And I'm not talking about a one-man team. Go on, I'll let you know when you can come back."

Thomas lowered his eyes to the ground and shuffled off without another word, staring at the ground the whole way across the field until he got to the bench. He jammed his rear-end down on the bench and crossed his arms. And pouted. "Huh," he said under his breath.

The practice was about to end. Thomas felt desperate. He wanted to play more than anything. He saw the coach round the corner and come his way. Thomas wouldn't look at him. "You ready to play the ball to your teammates too?"

Thomas didn't move a muscle.

"If not," Hackl continued. "Stay off the field."

Thomas's face turned red. He was angry, but he knew his coach was right.

Hackl studied Thomas for a moment, then turned and walked away.

Thomas looked up. "Coach, wait," he said and stood up. "I'm sorry."

"I don't want your apology, Muller, I want you to know what to do out there on the field, and think about the way you play," Hackl said.

Thomas remembered what Hackl had said about excuses, that in good sportsmanship, they were unnecessary and irritating. "I need to play with my teammates. I can't do it all by myself," he replied.

Hackl grinned at him. "Good answer. Go on, get out there."

Thomas nodded and hurried off to join his teammates. Hackl was pleased he had finally got through to the boy.

Minutes later, Thomas kicked the ball to Seppi and moved into an empty space between the opposing midfielders. Seppi flicked the ball to him from behind and he was in the right place to score another goal.

Hackl scratched his head and turned to his assistant coach. "Fast learner," he said. "I didn't teach him that."

"He doesn't watch where the other guys are, he watches where they're not, looking for space for himself," the other coach said.

"He's very mature," Hackl said and then sighed. "We better enjoy him while we can."

His assistant chuckled. "Aren't you getting a little ahead of yourself? He's only seven."

Hackl shook his head. "We'll keep him until we can't. But that kid is going places."

A lot of cheering grabbed their attention. Thomas had just scored another goal.

After practice, when Thomas came off the pitch, his father was there instead of his mother, standing beside the family car, smiling.

"Papa!" Thomas said and rushed into his father's arms.

Gerhard Muller squeezed his son tight, confused because his son was shuddering in his arms. "What's wrong?"

Thomas looked up at his father and Gerhard saw his son's face streaked with tears. "Nothing," Thomas said.

Gerhard gave him another squeeze. "You can tell me on the way."

That got Thomas's attention. "On the way? On the way to where?"

"It's a surprise," Gerhard replied with a grin.

Thomas spent the next hour telling his father about ball hogging and sitting on the bench and finally trying to get the secret out of him, but Gerhard's resolve was stronger. They got to Munich and pulled onto Säbener Strasse. Up ahead was a guarded gate and, beyond that, a gray multi-storied building as square as a Lego-made box. His father stopped his car at the gate and told the guard his name.

"Welcome to FC Bayern, Mr. Muller," the guard said and let them pass.

Just like that, Thomas realized they were at the FC Bayern Youth Academy. And they must have known they were coming because they knew who they were.

"What are we doing here, Papa?" Thomas asked, half in shock.

"There's someone I want you to meet," his father replied.

CHAPTER 7

THE AUTOGRAPH

Thomas was always three moves ahead of everyone else on the pitch. It was something that came to him naturally. Instinctually, he'd understood the geometry of the field ever since he was five. When he played for TSV Pähl, that's how he was able to always appear out of nowhere in the penalty area and the goal box, surprising everyone. He wondered why the coaches made such a big deal out of it. Wasn't that what he was supposed to do? Lots of players do it. His soccer heroes all did it. Gerd Muller did it. That's who he'd learned it from. Three moves. He stared at the Lego-looking box with windows that was the FC Bayern Munich Youth Academy building in awe.

He thought about what he had learned from the bench earlier in the day. It was easy to hog the ball. And it was hard to be a team player. He rolled down the car window and sucked in a breath. The city of Munich was so different from his village, so big and full of movement and noise. He tucked in his number 13 Muller jersey while his father parked the car and got out.

The FC Bayern second team was out on the field playing a scrimmage. Thomas ran ahead of his father and gripped the fence with both hands and watched the *real* players train. But then his eyes rested on the trainer.

He couldn't believe it.

It was Gerd Muller. Signing autographs.

"It's him!" he said to his dad in a shaky voice.

"Yes, it is," his dad said. "The best striker ever."

Thomas nodded.

"Someday, you could be playing for him," Gerhard said to his son.

"Really?"

"Yes," his father said. "If you work hard, it will happen."

One-two-three, Thomas thought. One to get ready. Two to go. Three to meet his hero. He hesitated. He was scared. And there he was. Suddenly close. There was a small group of boys near the sideline, watching Muller. Thomas was like a racehorse, champing at the bit to get the race on.

His father noticed and pushed him through the gate. "Go," he said.

Thomas started to go, then stopped himself and turned back, his heart racing. "May I run, Papa?" Thomas asked.

Gerhard grinned. "As fast as you can, son!"

Thomas took off before his father had finished speaking and raced to where Gerd Muller was signing autographs.

"Sorry, kids, I'm out of cards," Gerd Muller said, showing them the palms of his hands.

Thomas stood motionless. He was so disappointed. He was too late.

Gerd Muller waved goodbye and walked away toward the parking lot.

Thomas, turned, dejected, and shuffled back to where his father was waiting for him near the stands.

"What happened?" Gerhard asked.

"He ran out of cards and left," Thomas mumbled, head down.

Gerhard looked over at the parking lot where Gerd Muller was opening his car door, then turned back to his son. "So, you give up?"

Thomas looked at his father and fought back the tears. "No," he said.

Gerhard put his hand on his son's shoulder. "Look. He's getting in his car. Go over there and tell him how much you like him."

Thomas's face lit up. "Really?"

"You better hurry, before he leaves."

Thomas's eyes widened, and he raced off toward the parking lot as fast as he could run.

Muller was just getting behind the wheel of his car when Thomas ran up. "Mr. Muller!"

Gerd Muller looked up and flashed a smile when he saw Thomas.

"I – I – y-you're my favorite player," Thomas said breathlessly.

Gerd Muller saw Thomas was wearing his number 13 jersey. "What's your name, son?"

Thomas blurted out, "Thomas Muller, sir!" He was more excited than he had ever felt in his life.

"Muller, huh?" Gerd said grinned. "What do you know! It's Muller again!"

"Yes, sir!" Thomas replied and handed him his notepad and pen. "Please may I have your autograph?"

"It's a good thing you caught me here. I ran out of cards on the field, but I have plenty in the car." He flashed a card and wrote a note to Thomas, signed it, and handed it to him. "What do you play, Thomas Muller?"

"Everything!"

Gerd Muller laughed and ruffled Thomas's hair. "That's how you become great. But no ball hogging, right? There's a whole team out there you need to support."

Thomas's jaw dropped and his eyes grew as wide as twin full moons in August. "N-no, sir! No ball hogging."

"Good, good, keep up the good work, Muller! I hope to see you here, someday!" He turned the key and started the engine.

"Sir?" Thomas shouted over the engine noise. Gerd Muller looked up at him from behind the wheel of his car.

"How did you know I was a ball hog?" Thomas asked.

Gerd Muller laughed again. It was a full hearty laugh that drew Thomas in. "I didn't," he said and put the car in gear. "But all the great ones are, in the beginning!" With that, he backed out of his parking place and drove away.

Thomas and his father spent the rest of the day watching the FC Bayern squads practice and go through their drills. They left when the sun went down. Most of the way home, Thomas could not take his eyes off his Gerd Muller autograph. He finally had a real one. He told his father the story nine different ways until he fell asleep in the middle of a sentence.

When they arrived home, Thomas was fast asleep, so Gerhard carried his son inside and put him to bed in the bed with FC Bayern sheets and an FC Bayern quilt. He kissed him on the forehead and took a look around the room. The walls were covered in posters of FC Bayern superstars. Lothar Matthäus watched him from the right, Mehmet Scholl from the left, Mario Basler from behind, and Gerd Muller faced him. Gerhard turned out the light and closed the door.

CHAPTER 8

THE HERO, THE CASTLE, AND THE PLAY

Thomas, his father, his mother, his brother Simon, his cousins, and his grandmother crowded on the couch and watched the final of the 1996 Euros on TV, broadcast live from Wembley Stadium in England. Germany was playing the Czech Republic. The score was one to one, five minutes into the first extra-time period. Forty-two minutes earlier, Oliver Bierhoff had come in as a substitute and scored their only goal, equalizing the score.

Thomas jumped to his feet. "Germany!" he shouted his arms waving wildly.

Then it happened. Oliver Bierhoff, the number 20 forward, moved into position, covered by defender Miroslav Kadlec. Jurgen Klinsmann flicked the ball to him. Bierhoff whirled around Kadlec, intercepted the ball, and left-footed it into the right side of the net.

Goal!!!

Thomas jumped as high as he could. The entire room was on their feet cheering until their voices were hoarse.

On the pitch, Bierhoff ripped off his jersey and screamed with delight.

Then the Italian assistant referee lifted his orange flag. The referee hadn't seen the error. The Czech coach stood next to the linesman with the orange flag.

"Offside?" everyone cried out.

"Offside?" Thomas muttered.

The Muller living room grew silent.

Thomas moaned. His grandmother said, "Shhh!"

"It is the German striker Stefan Kuntz," the television announcer said.

The referee ran over to his assistant and shook his head, no.

The goal stood.

The Mullers were all on their feet again, screaming for joy.

Germany had won the Euros, thanks to Oliver Bierhoff and Jurgen Klinsmann.

Thomas grabbed his father by the face and kissed him.

A few days later, Thomas tacked up a poster of Oliver Bierhoff alongside Gerd Muller's poster on the wall behind his bed, and Bierhoff joined the wall of heroes in his bedroom.

Thomas had many relatives and many friends in Pähl. One Saturday morning, on a day off from practice when there was no match at TSV Pähl, he got up at the crack of dawn and raced up the hill to the High Castle to hook up with his friend and fellow TSV Pähl player, Philip Stauffenberg.

The pond near the High Castle of Pähl was frozen and Thomas knew it was going to be a fun day.

The High Castle, built in the 1880s and constructed of solid stone atop a hill a hundred yards above Oberdorf, was surrounded by a dense green forest. It was a real noble residence in the old Bavarian style of turrets and towers. The fancy gate was just up the street from where Thomas's parents had built their home. From high atop the main tower, one could see Unterdorf and Oberdorf as well as a 360-degree view of the countryside and the Bavarian Alps. From the village of Pähl below, looking up, the castle was nothing short of magic. For Thomas and his friends, it was nothing but pure fun.

He stepped out on the frozen pond. It was always fascinating how the water became ice, and he loved how the ice felt beneath his skates.

He swung his hockey stick at the polished stone they used as a puck as it skittered across the ice in front of him, but instead of whacking it into the makeshift goal, he tripped himself with it.

WHAM!

He sprawled face-first and skidded across the ice. His friend, Philip, was right in front of him and coming at him fast, so he squeezed his eyes shut and hoped for the best. He rolled into Philip, knocking him down, and the momentum sent both boys spinning across the ice and crashing into the snowdrift at the north end of the pond. Moments later, their heads popped out from under the newly fallen snow, one-by-one, and they laughed as they spit the white stuff out. Their eyebrows were caked with ice and they looked like Santa's elves.

"Oops!" Thomas said as he crawled out of the snow cave. Philip, still buried in the snow, laughed, and his laugh echoed over the pond. Thomas pulled him out.

Bettina Stauffenberg, statuesque and strikingly beautiful, stood on a high porch and watched the boys play hockey on the frozen pond. She was the owner of High Castle.

Philip saw her first. He had skated off and sat on a rock, taking off his skates. Thomas skated over to him and walked in the muddy grass to where Philip was seated.

"Your mom is watching us," Thomas said.

"Yes," Philip replied. "I think she wants me to come in."

Both boys walked toward the castle. Philip's mother was the librarian for the nearby Catholic church as well as the self-proclaimed historian of Pähl. The townsfolk called her Chatelaine because she was the woman who owned this chateau. They reached the steps leading up to the castle. Thomas picked up his backpack and slung it over his shoulder, along with his skates.

"Did you bring a ball?" Philip asked.

Thomas patted his bag. "Don't leave home without it."

Philip flashed a grin.

The courtyard of the castle worked great as a soccer pitch. Fun in the summer, but a bit dangerous in the winter because of the ice. Thomas and Philip decided to have a one-on-one match. Thomas dropped the ball and, while it bounced, he flicked it over Philip's head and into the dry-stone fountain up against the north wall of the castle.

The hard dirt and dying grass-covered courtyard was riddled with patches of dangerous black ice and Philip skidded sideways on it like he was moon-walking when he charged after the ball. He managed to get to the bone-dry fountain without slipping and snatched the ball up and let it drop to the dirt, then chased it before he could hit it again. Thomas slipped-and-slid, but stole the ball and lobbed it into the fountain again.

After six goals, Philip gave up.

"I quit!" Philip cried out. "You never let me score!"

"It's not my fault!" Thomas replied.

"Yeah well, maybe you should let me win sometimes!" Philip pleaded.

Thomas stopped and looked at his friend. "Yeah, maybe I should," he said. "But you know I can't."

Philip nodded. You would have to be crazy to let someone else win.

Then it was time to go home.

Thomas gathered his kit and walked alone down the winding road to the gate that led to Oberdorf and beyond, up the road, to his home, keeping his ball close to his foot the whole way, practicing his dribbling.

School was back in session and Thomas had turned eight. Mrs. Hupfauf walked up and down the aisles of desks, returning tests. "Perfect score, Thomas," she said. "Best in the class." She dropped the paper on his desk. There were a few groans from around the room from jealous students. Thomas was happy.

When she was finished handing out test results, Mrs. Hupfauf brought Thomas up to the front of the class. "I have chosen Thomas to play the lead in our play by the great German comedian Karl Valentin. I chose him not only because he is tall like a fence rail, just like Mr. Valentin, but also because he likes to make jokes and interrupt the class, so I assumed this was his way of trying out for the part."

Thomas giggled and the rest of the class shared his laugh. "Good choice, Mrs. Hupfauf," he said. More laughs.

"But we need an understudy," she said. No one knew what an understudy was, so she explained. "It is someone who can step in and do the part if Thomas can't. I was thinking of your cousin, Stephan Gemander," Mrs. Hupfauf said to Thomas.

Stephan's eyes grew wide like saucers. "I... I can't be in a play! I'm too scared!" he said from the back of the room.

"We won't need an under... uh, you know, Mrs. Hupfauf," Thomas jumped in. "I can do it all by myself," he said.

Stephan blew out a breath of relief and slumped back down on his desk.

"Very well," Mrs. Hupfauf said. "We will be doing *In der Apotheke*, a play based on a short film made by Hans Albin in 1941. Mr. Valentin goes to the pharmacy for his wife."

There were lots of snickers from around the room.

"It's funny already?" Mrs. Hupfauf asked.

"They think it's funny I have a wife," Thomas explained.

Mrs. Hupfauf chuckled. "Well, anyway, he goes to the pharmacy to pick up some medicine but by the time he gets there he's forgotten what he is supposed to get, so the pharmacist asks him to describe how the patient feels in order to know which medicine to give him. Can you play Mr. Valentin, Thomas?" she asked.

Thomas stood up. "I sure can, Mrs. Hupfauf." And without further ado, he started hacking loudly, grabbed his throat with both hands like he was choking himself, then fell over Seppi's desk, spilling both boys into the aisle.

The class erupted in laughter.

Thomas looked up from the floor with a broad smile. "How was that?"

Mrs. Hupfauf crossed her arms and grinned. "It's a start," she said.

CHAPTER 9

THE GOLDEN SEASON

At four in the afternoon, an hour and a half before the match at TSV Pähl, Thomas cleaned up the locker room and put away all the equipment. A man stood in the doorway, unknown to Thomas, and watched with amusement. The training grounds were deserted. The man disappeared from the doorway as Thomas ran out with a ball and hurried onto the pitch. He dropped the ball on the turf and ran the field ten times, dribbling the ball from one foot to the other, up and down, side to side. When he was done, he dropped and did twenty pushups. Then he did one deep knee bend. Then he and did nineteen pushups and two deep knee bends. He did not stop until he did one pushup and twenty deep knee bends. Two hundred and twelve each. He never made a sound other than his own breathing and grunting.

"Impressive!" the man who had been watching him clean up the locker room shouted to him from the sideline.

Thomas looked up. He had never seen him before. "Hello, sir," he said. He walked over to the man and held out his hand. "Thomas Muller."

"So, I have been told," the man said, shaking the ten-year-old's hand, never letting go. "You're early. I'm Coach Klapheck"

"Yes Coach, I like to be prepared," Thomas said.

"Call me Dieter," he said. "Boy, you have a strong grip," he added, looking at his hand.

"I do a lot of pushups," Thomas replied.

"Yes, I noticed that," Dieter said.

Thomas grinned. "Thanks for noticing."

Dieter smiled broadly "Can I ask you something?"

"Yes sir," Thomas replied.

"I also noticed you in the locker room, cleaning up the equipment from the last practice."

"Yes, sir," Thomas replied.

"So how come you don't do that at home?"

Thomas's eyes widened. He turned beet red and was mortified. "H-how did you know that?"

Dieter grinned. "This is Pähl," he said with a wink. "Everyone knows everything. Let's get back to work, huh? Our game is going to be here before we know it!"

"Yes, sir!" Thomas said.

"And thanks for showing up early. Hard work always pays off." With that, he walked off.

An hour and a half later, the stands were half-full and the match was on. The crowd leaped to its feet and cheered Thomas as he charged from the middle to the left, two steps ahead of his teammates, intercepted the ball, and took it downfield as three boys swarmed all over him. He kicked the ball into the net between the goalkeeper's hands and it was one to zero in the first five minutes.

The crowd was back on their feet, cheering wildly.

Thomas scored ten goals in that match and Pähl won decisively. And so, a golden season began for him.

The start of the season saw only a smattering of townsfolk in the stands, mostly the families of the players. But, after Thomas's sixtieth goal, word got out around Pähl about their homegrown kid having a golden season and it was not long before the stands were packed full for every match. TSV Pähl was heading for the championship and Thomas was heading for his 120th goal.

Thomas's family was always there in the stands: mom, dad, grandma, and Simon. Next to them were the cousins with whom Thomas had played pick-up games ever since they had learned how to walk.

Also, in the stands, sitting elsewhere, were Norbert Scholz, the shopkeeper, his wife Rosemarie, and their daughter. Whenever Thomas scored, the shopkeeper leaped to his feet with a *Mickey Mouse* comic in each hand and waved them like flags. Next to him on the bench was a short stack of comic books and a small basket of chocolate, all to present to his favorite customer – and soccer player – after the game. The window of his shop was covered in pictures of soccer balls and photographs of Thomas.

Thomas saw Mr. Scholz in the stands and smiled broadly.

Down the row sat Philip Stauffenberg's mother Bettina, who had come all the way down the hill from her castle to watch her son and his best friend. His teacher, Mrs. Hupfauf, was also there to see her star pupil and the star of her new play; and so was his

Kindergarten teacher, Margret Hager, who wouldn't let him play soccer because it was against the rules, even though Thomas could outplay any boy in town three years his senior.

In Pähl, everyone knew everyone else's business, and everyone was in love with the beautiful game. And their local hero, Thomas Muller.

Word got out all over the districts of Bavaria that there was a ten-year-old kid at TSV Pähl who stood out. He scored double digits in almost every match. Everyone in town and their friends and family came to see him play.

So did the sports agents.

The 1998/99 season at TSV Pähl started out with a bang and never let up. Even before it was over, the team had won the championship. Total goals scored: 175. One hundred twenty of them were by Thomas alone. The rest were scored mostly by Seppi.

Near the end of the season, a scout from SpVgg Unterhaching hesitated when he walked up the row of seats and sat next to a man he knew. A scout from 1860 Munchen. They nodded uncomfortably to each other. They assumed they were both there for the same reason. The man from 1860 had a notepad out and was writing quickly. The scout from SpVgg sighed and took out his own notepad and they both laughed at the situation. That's when someone nearby cleared his throat. They both looked up in unison as the scout from Bayern Munich sat down next to them and also took out a notepad. "Well, I guess I know why we are all here," the Bayern scout said.

The crowd cheered. Out on the field, Thomas Muller had just scored another goal.

"Him," the scout from FC Bayern said, indicating Thomas.

"It's crazy how good he is," the scout from 1860 Munchen said.

"*How* old did they say he was?" asked the scout from SpVgg Unterhaching.

"Just ten," said the scout from Bayern.

"Not bad," the scout from 1860 Munchen said. "He is probably ready to move up to D."

The scout from FC Bayern stood up unexpectedly as if to leave. "Whenever D was short at Pähl, he filled in." He started to leave. Not to be outdone, the other two stood up and blocked him. "What's the rush, Jan?" the scout from 1860 teased.

The scout from Bayern was Jan Pienta.

"Does Mrs. Pienta have something special on the table for supper tonight?" the scout from Unterhaching teased. The men laughed, then quickly left in three different directions.

They all circled the kid's name.

They all would report back what they'd just seen.

CHAPTER 10

HARD DECISIONS

A few months later, as the world ushered in a new century, Jan Pienta, the scout from FC Bayern, stood in his row in the wooden stands. He watched the pitch, transfixed, as Thomas Muller charged downfield, shot the ball to a left midfielder, then seemed to disappear and re-appear near the goal in a space the size of a phone booth, just as the ball was flicked back to him. He tapped the ball into the left side of the net, scoring his first goal of the semi-final match of the Merkur Cup for TSV Pähl.

"Nice," Pienta muttered and sat down.

"OW!"

He looked back. He had just sat down on Norbert Scholz. He jumped up like a wild animal had just bit him. "I beg your pardon!" Pienta said. "I am so sorry. I... I didn't see you."

Scholz grinned and his wife smiled at the scout. "Your eyes were on the striker," Mrs. Scholz said. "We don't blame you. He's quite good. Family friend. That is why we are here. To watch Thomas."

Pienta smiled. "How delightful," he said. The couple smelled of fresh bread and, when he sat down next to Norbert, it was like he was in a bakery.

Norbert stuck out his hand. "Norbert Scholz. We own a little bakery shop in Pähl."

"A bakery," Pienta said.

"That and other things," Mrs. Scholz said. "Thomas buys his chocolate and his comic books from us."

Pienta stuck out his hand. "Jan Pienta."

"The Bayern scout, yes, I know," Norbert said with a wink and a shrug. "I saw your picture in the paper the other day. Oh! How rude of me! I would like you to meet Thomas's parents, Klaudia and Gerhard," he said, and that was when Pienta noticed the couple on the other side of them. Klaudia waved. "Hello," she said just as Simon leaned forward and came into view. "And this is Thomas's younger brother, Simon."

Pienta nodded, then smiled to himself and chuckled. "And here I thought I was on a top-secret mission to spy on your son," he said and shook first Klaudia's hand, then Gerhard's, then little Simon's.

The crowd leaped to their feet all around him and cheered wildly and Pienta was on his feet and not sure why.

"He just scored again," Norbert explained.

"I think you brought him luck, Mr. Pienta," Gerhard said.

Pienta chuckled and sat back down. Pienta ran the scouting department for the FC Bayern Youth Program and was well-known to local soccer fans. His home turf back in Munich was the youth field and the Lego building on the Bayern grounds Thomas had visited some years ago.

He had taken a look at Thomas when he was ending his season at TSV Pähl and he wanted to take another look during the Merkur.

It was a new century and Pienta already felt it would get off to a good start. He had a good feeling about what he could and would accomplish this year. There were a number of boys from all around Bavaria, all born in what was turning out to a magical, golden year: 1989. Ten years later, in the new century, they were ready for level D. Thomas was just the start.

Downfield, Dieter stared at the man who had just joined the Muller family in the stands. He recognized him immediately. "Uh-oh," he muttered and nudged Peter Hackl. "Look who just dropped in for a visit."

Hackl checked him out. "It's Pienta. The scout from Bayern. What's he doing here? Did we do something right for a change?"

Dieter chuckled at the joke then his face fell when he realized. "Afraid so. He must be here to see Muller."

Hackl sighed. "Well, we always knew this day would come. Thomas is ready for D, anyway," he said and looked at the field then back to the man in the stands. "I'm grateful for the time we had him. It will hurt to lose him, but it's the right thing to do."

Jan Pienta moved past Scholz and sat down next to Klaudia, Thomas's mom, who made room for him. Then Thomas scored another goal and Pienta leaped to his feet. "I love his energy. He's moving all the time," he said to her, and she nodded. Just then, the crowd roared and were on their feet again. Pienta looked one way then the other, then joined the rest of the crowd and stood up just as Thomas skidded out of the box on his knees after scoring another goal and the rest of teammates piled on top of him.

"Eight goals!" Simon announced and puffed out his chest. "That's his eighth goal in the Merkur!"

A few minutes later, the match was over. Someone got on the loudspeaker and asked that everyone remain seated, it was now time for the boys to participate in the *Goal-Shooting Contest*.

Pienta was quite excited. "I have to admit. Your boy has it in him," he said to Gerhard and Klaudia. "I want to bring him to our youth program at Bayern."

Gerhard's eyes widened. "That's marvelous!" he said trying to conceal his excitement. When the scout left, he turned to his wife. She wasn't happy.

"What's wrong?" he asked.

"Well, *I* have to admit, I don't like it very much," Klaudia said. Then she raised an eyebrow and crossed her arms. Her face had gone all cloudy.

"What is it?" Gerhard asked. Whenever she did that, it meant something was bothering her.

"Going to Munich and back will be difficult for Thomas," she said.

"Yes, that's true," Gerhard said, unsure of where she was going with this. "And?" he asked.

"And I don't want him to go," Klaudia replied.

A few days later, Thomas stood in the wings of the elementary school stage, all wound-up and nervous, waiting for his cue to go on. He peeked through the curtain and saw that every seat was filled. He saw his family taking up one whole row.

He took a deep breath.

The curtain came up. The stage was wrapped in the painted backdrop of a pharmacy. There was a wooden counter stage left, and a girl dressed in a white coat was behind it. The bell on a door sounded offstage and Thomas entered and crossed over to the pharmacist behind the counter.

Gerhard and Klaudia and the rest of the family applauded.

"May I help you, sir?" the pharmacist asked.

"I need some medicine for my child," Thomas replied loudly.

Simon snickered then turned to his mother. "He said he has a child," he whispered and Klaudia elbowed him to be quiet.

"Yes, sir," the pharmacist said. "What medicine is it that you need?"

Thomas thought about it for a moment. "Isopropil-prophemil-barbitursauresphenil-dimethyl-dimenthyl-aminophirazolon," he said, then paused. "I think," he added.

The pharmacist gave him a funny look and the audience burst out in uproarious laughter.

The laughter helped Thomas lose his stage fright, and he relaxed into his role. The rest of the one-act play went very well. The pharmacist had never heard of that chemical and asked Thomas to describe the symptoms and Thomas acted them out in pure Karl Valentin slapstick comedy. The audience adored him. His friends and family were surprised that he was even up there on stage, let alone entertaining them. After the performance, Thomas stood out in front of the auditorium and shook the hands of the admirers in the audience and was hugged by every member of his family.

Although Thomas's family were on pins and needles waiting for the call from Pienta about Bayern, Thomas was focused on the Merkur Cup finals in Markt-Schwaben, a village 25 miles from Munich, also in the Bavarian district of Oberbayern. His team had already won their district semi-finals, but then the team found itself up against the likes of SpVgg Unterhaching, TSV 1860 Munchen, and finally FC Bayern Munich, and the best TSV Pähl could do was sixth place. Bayern won the Cup. On the field, after the match, Klapheck touched Hackl's arm.

"Look who's coming," he said.

"Oh, I can't believe it!" Hackl said. "Thomas's father."

"Do you think he wants to congratulate us for getting sixth place?" Klapheck asked with a wry smile.

"No. I do not," Hackl said. "I think it's something we anticipated for a long time." Gerhard Muller approached them and shook their hands.

"You probably know why I'm here," he said. "You've done a terrific job with the team and especially with one young player with whom I share something personal," he said with a chuckle.

"Besides your last name?" quipped Hackl.

Gerhard chuckled. "It's time to take my son to the next level," he said, nodding toward Thomas still on the pitch. Hackl bit his lip. "I am going to need Thomas's player's license."

Hackl looked at Klapheck. The moment they dreaded had finally arrived. Thomas Muller was moving up to Bayern. Hackl looked at his shoes. "We'll get it for you," Klapheck said.

"I'll break the news to him," Hackl said.

In the locker room after the match, Thomas changed. On the way out, Peter Hackl was waiting for him. "Can we talk?" he asked.

Thomas was surprised to see him waiting there. "What did I do?"

Hackl laughed and ruffled his hair. "Every time someone looks at you funny, you think something is wrong. You played brilliantly. Let's take a walk, then I'll let your family have you."

Thomas smiled and nodded.

Minutes later, they were walking around the field. "My dream for you – actually all of our dreams for you – was to move you all up to level D this year. That's what happens if you stay and you turn eleven."

"I'm moving up?!" Thomas was excited.

Hackl took a long time to find the rest of his words. "Yes, Thomas. You're moving up…"

"That's fantastic!" he jumped in before Hackl could finish his sentence.

"But not with us."

"What?"

"Yes, you are leaving us. But that is because you are going to play for Bayern."

Thomas realized what his coach had just said and stopped. Hackl watched his prodigy's face gradually move from a terrible frown to an ecstatic smile.

"For real?" Thomas asked.

"I'm a selfish coach, Thomas. So, I wish it wasn't true. But it is. It's for real."

Thomas took a deep breath, then hugged his coach tighter than he'd ever hugged anyone before. He could tell by the look on his coach's face that this was really happening. "It's true! I'm going to Bayern! I can't believe it!" He wiped the tears from his eyes.

He wanted badly to break the news to his parents.

That was when his mother and father came down out of the stands with the FC Bayern scout, Jan Pienta, and joined them. Thomas ran to his mother and hugged her tight. "Oh Mama, I can't believe it! I'm going to Bayern!" he shouted. Then he moved to his father and hugged him too. Then he hugged Simon and picked him up off the ground and spun him around.

"Not so fast," Klaudia said and all the joy went out of Thomas's face. Hackl's too.

"He's only eleven years old. He has school to finish and Munich is over 30 miles away. He's never been away from home in his life," she said.

"I completely understand, Mrs. Muller," Pienta said. "We have thought about this and I'll tell you what. For Thomas's first year, you bring him to Munich once a week and he plays for us. The rest of the week, he stays here and plays for TSV Pähl. We let him get acclimated to the new team. I know he's been with friends here at Pähl for most of his life and the change in teams and location is no small move. So, we give it a year and see how it goes. If he likes it, he stays. If not, he can decide what to do."

Klaudia could not believe it. She thought this was a very gracious and thoughtful offer. She turned to Gerhard. "It sounds too good to be true," she whispered to him, loud enough for Pienta to hear and he chuckled.

"That is a very good offer," Gerhard remarked.

Pienta nodded. "We really want him. And for us, family is more important than anything else. We are not in this for the short game. We're in it for the long haul," he said.

Gerhard turned to Thomas. "What do you think?"

"So, I only get to go once a week?" He sounded disappointed. "On the train?"

"Yes," Pienta said. "But you will play for the new D Youth squad we are developing, and you'll also be available for our matches."

Thomas flashed a grin. "Yes!"

Klaudia saw how happy he was and linked her arm in her husband's then thrust out her right hand to Pienta. "You have a deal."

Just like that, Thomas was going to Bayern.

Later that night, the Mullers had a houseful of family for a celebration.

Everyone was at the dinner table, playing cards. Thomas looked at his partner, Simon, and they compared hands. He turned to the rest of the table. "Schneider!" Thomas shouted and threw down his cards on the table. They were having a family tournament playing Thomas's favorite card game, Sheepshead, and he and his partner had just got the required thirty-one points to win the trick. The entire family was packed into the living room, sitting at one long table that stretched from one end of the room to the other. Everyone was there – brothers and sisters, aunts and uncles, and cousins; twenty-five of them. Most of them just watched, but everyone's heart was in the game.

Gerhard groaned and let his cards flutter to the table. "The boys are too good for us!"

"I have a better idea," Klaudia said coming in from the kitchen to the rescue, carrying trays of food. She was followed by her mother, who was also carrying a tray of food. "Let's eat. It's not every day someone in the Muller family gets to play for FC Bayern!"

They raised a toast to Thomas's late grandfather.

"I wish he could have lived to see this moment," Grandma said, tearing up. "He is so proud of you up there in heaven," she said.

"I swear, I won't let him down," Thomas said and hugged his grandma. "I'll score a lot of goals for Bayern – and for him."

They hugged and everyone cheered.

CHAPTER 11
BAYERN YOUTH

Thomas walked out of the front door of his house and stopped at the family car. His mother was behind the wheel. She was going to drive him to the Bayern Youth field in Munich for his weekly practice. It was only a little over 30 miles away but, to him, it felt like he was going far away.

He had worn a number 13 jersey since he was five years old and had dreamed of playing for Bayern for as long as he could remember.

And now the big day had arrived.

He opened the passenger door and his mother looked up at him.

"Ready to play for Bayern?"

Thomas cracked a big smile.

"Ready," he said excitedly.

An hour later, Klaudia pulled up to the Bayern Youth facility and stopped. Thomas quickly opened the door, grabbed his kit bag, jumped out, and hurried around to the driver's side window. His mother looked worried.

"What's wrong?" he asked.

Klaudia took a deep breath. "Nothing, honey. It's just your first time so far away without us.

"It's just one day a week," Thomas replied.

Klaudia managed a smile.

Thomas hugged her through the window. "I'll see you tonight," he said.

Klaudia nodded. "See you tonight."

Half an hour later, he lined up on the field with the rest of his squad. He hurriedly moved next to a boy his own age with sandy blond hair who was slightly shorter than him. The boy looked over and stuck out his hand. "Viktor," the boy said. "Viktor Bopp."

Thomas nodded, scared out of his wits but trying to hide it. "Thomas," he managed to get out. Viktor had an accent and when he saw Thomas think about it, he answered for him. "I'm from Ukraine. There he is," he whispered, jerking his head toward the building as a stocky man with red hair and beard came marching their way.

"Who?" Thomas whispered back.

"Our trainer," Viktor whispered. "Heiko Vogel."

Vogel stopped in front of his boys and grinned broadly. "I love this game," he said. "How about you?"

All the boys nodded and acknowledged their love for the game.

"You want to hear something funny? Every one of you plays better than I ever could or would. And you're only ten years old!"

There was laughter all around, from the boys and from the coaching staff.

"That's because I didn't come to Bayern by way of being a great player like you. Oh, I played a little. But I wasn't any good. So, I studied Sports Science." He waited for a moment. "And that is how – and that is why – we are going to win."

The boys cheered.

Thomas thought he was cool.

"All right, let's go!" Vogel said. He blew his whistle, and the boys hit the field for the first time together.

Later they had a little scrimmage.

Thomas noticed that Viktor was never exactly where he should be when he passed him the ball.

"Sorry," Viktor said, breathless.

"That's okay, you watch me," Thomas said. With his help, Viktor improved.

Vogel watched with interest. He asked Thomas to move forward, kept Viktor in the middle, and put Philipp Lahm and Mats Hummels with Thomas. He was evaluating them, trying to figure out their strengths and weaknesses. Most of all, their game intelligence. For the players, it was about starting to learn the game from scratch and forgetting a lot of what they thought they knew about it.

It was just the first day.

Gerhard was waiting in the car for Thomas when he rushed up. It was time to go home. He climbed in and closed the door. "How did it go?" Gerhard asked.

Thomas grinned. "I can't wait for next week."

Thomas did not sleep a wink that night.

Over the next year, Thomas, Philipp, and Mats were inseparable on the field and, with Vogel's guidance, they perfected their plays. But Thomas's favorite training pal was just one guy – Viktor Bopp. Thomas was anything but shy when it came to playing on a new squad with all his new teammates. He dove in headfirst, just like he did with everything in life. It was like that, once a week for what seemed like forever. Klaudia dropped him off after school and Gerhard picked him up after work in the early evening. Thomas loved driving home with his father because they talked a lot about the games.

Thomas knew he would soon have to make a decision whether to stay with Bayern or not. He didn't want to think about it, he was having too much fun and had made some really good friends.

One night at home when he and his father were watching a soccer match, the phone rang. Thomas saw his mother answer it in the kitchen and her face looked worried.

"What's wrong, Mama?" Thomas asked, afraid it was bad news.

Klaudia's eyes met her husband's, then drifted to Thomas. "Nothing is wrong, son," she said and offered him the phone.

Thomas got up, went into the kitchen, and took the phone. He put it to his ear, but he was afraid to speak so he just stood there in silence.

"Say something," Klaudia said.

"Hello?" Thomas asked into the receiver. He listened while someone spoke to him.

It was the manager of the youth program at *1860 Munich*, the other Bundesliga club in Munich.

"We want you to play for us, Thomas," the man on the phone said to him.

Thomas looked over at his mother as his father joined them in the kitchen along with his brother Simon. They all stared at him waiting for him to say something. "It's the Blues," he whispered, cupping the phone with one hand so the man at the other end of the line could not hear him. They were called the "Blues" because their home kit was blue and white. "They want me to play for them."

Gerhard looked at Klaudia and Klaudia looked at Gerhard.

There was a long, loud silence in the kitchen. The only noise was the sound of a crowd cheering on the TV.

"What are you going to tell them?" Gerhard asked him.

"Don't you think he's too young to make that kind of decision?" Klaudia asked.

Thomas looked at his family and shushed them with his eyes, then returned to the phone conversation. "I'm sorry, sir, but I'm already playing for FC Bayern," he said.

There was a long pause as Thomas listened, then he hung up the phone.

And said nothing.

"Well?" Klaudia asked. "What did he say?"

"He thanked me for my time and wished me well."

Klaudia and Gerhard looked at each other and smiled. "Proud of you son," Gerhard said. His mother hugged him.

"Cool, Thom," Simon said and hugged him.

Thomas was proud of himself too. For the first time in his life, he felt like he was growing up.

On the last day of his first year at Bayern, Heiko Vogel was waiting for him when he came off the field after practice. It was a Friday. "Let's talk."

Together, they walked around the field, following the perimeter lines.

"I don't know if you know this or not, Thom, but once upon a time, I was on a committee here at Bayern. We had heard about you and we voted unanimously to send Jan Pienta out to TSV Pähl to scout you."

Thomas was surprised. And moved. It was one of the nicest things anyone had ever said to him. "You know what day it is, Coach?" he asked.

Vogel looked at Thomas and smiled. "Friday?"

"Yes." Thomas laughed. "It's also the last day of my first year."

"Oh? Is it?" Vogel pretended not to know. "I've been so busy, I didn't realize that."

Thomas smiled. He liked to look people in the eye. His grandmother always said that the eyes were the windows to the soul and to always make eye contact. He knew why Coach Vogel had told him all that stuff about the committee and scouting him. They wanted him to stay. At that moment, he felt wanted and was proud to be a member of the Bayern organization. "Anyway, I just wanted to let you know that I'm staying."

Vogel's eyes lit up. "Are you sure?"

"Don't try to talk me out of it, Coach," Thomas said. "My grandfather would never forgive me if he thought I played for any other team."

Vogel laughed. "I called your father and told him how much we wanted you and I want to tell you. You're going to be a pro. You're going to make money playing soccer. I can't tell you how happy I am to tell you that."

"I'm pretty happy you told me that too, Coach," Thomas quipped.

Vogel smiled. "Then I'll see you on Monday."

"Yes, see you Monday." He shook Vogel's hand, and the team manager trotted away, leaving him alone on the field. He looked around and closed his eyes. He pictured his grandfather, in the stands, wearing his own threadbare Bayern jersey, jumping to his feet, hopping and cheering like a young man. Cheering wildly. For him.

CHAPTER 12
TRAINS AND TRAINING

The Mullers had a decision to make. Was Thomas old enough to travel on the train alone to Bayern and back? They decided to take a family vote.

"All in favor of Thomas being allowed to ride the train to Bayern, raise your hands," Klaudia said and looked around the dinner table. Thomas, Gerhard, and grandma all raised their hands. Simon didn't raise his hand.

"Opposed?"

Simon raised his hand, pretending not to care, glancing up at the ceiling so he did not have to meet his older brother's glare.

"Very funny," Thomas said and shoved him out of his chair and both boys wrestled around on the floor. Thomas won and pinned his younger brother. "Why don't you want me to go?"

"I want to go with you," Simon said.

Thomas loved his little brother. He would do anything for him. "Maybe, someday." He got up and stretched out his hand. Simon took it, and Thomas helped him up.

When Thomas and Simon sat back down at the table, mom, dad, and Erna were glaring at them in silence.

"Are you two quite finished?" Klaudia asked.

"Sorry, Mama," Simon said and resumed eating.

Thomas smiled. "Pass the potatoes?"

Thomas was finally on his own. The following Monday, he took the train alone. He loved it. The new system of getting him to and from FC Bayern was complex and needed to be memorized but, like a typical play on the pitch, Thomas was up to the challenge. It was all a matter of one-two-three.

"Are you sure you can remember all this? You don't want to take notes?" his grandmother asked.

"I already have all of it right up here, in a nutshell," Thomas replied, tapping the side of his head with his index finger.

She rolled her eyes at his joke.

He opened the door and got out of her car. That was the first leg of the journey. One, grandma drives him to the Tutzing Suburban train station. Two, he takes the Suburban to Munich Main Station. Three, change to the subway to Wettersteinplatz. Then a 10-minute walk to the training grounds.

"Piece of cake," he said and told her the route.

"And home?" she asked.

"Reverse steps one through three."

His grandmother smiled. "You forgot the part about your homework."

"Oh!" Thomas remembered. "And do my homework on the train so I can pass my *Arbitur* when I'm ready to graduate high school."

"Good boy," she said. "See you tonight."

Thomas watched her drive away. When she was out of sight, he felt a sudden sense of freedom he hadn't ever felt before.

He was twelve when he started going back and forth all by himself and he did the routine for two years. When he was fourteen, and legally old enough in Germany to be paid for his soccer skills, he was given a stipend. When people asked him how much he made he would say: "Not enough to live like a king, but more than zero."

The train came, and he climbed aboard. It was crowded, but he found his usual window seat, which was where he did his homework. It had been his seat for two years and he got a lot done in it.

He always knew when he got within a block of the training ground because he could smell the grass.

That's how it was every day of the week up to the end of 2003.

Practice, practice, and some more practice during the week and then matches on Saturdays.

One day, Thomas was training when he saw the group of men standing with his coach, Stephan Beckenbauer.

Mats Hummels stopped next to him. "Who are those guys?" Thomas asked.

Mats smiled at him, then nodded toward the two men chatting on the sideline with their coach. "One's the coach of the U16 national team and the other is an agent."

"Yeah?" Thomas was intrigued.

Mats looked at him. "Yeah. Bernd Stöber is the trainer of the U16 national team, that's the guy on the left, and Ludwig Kögl is a sports agent, the one on the right."

"How do you know so much?"

"I read *Kicker*," Mats replied. "And I don't just look at the pictures!"

The boys shared a laugh.

"Maybe we should show them some of our moves?" Thomas said.

Mats laughed. "Naw, they're not interested in me. They're only here to look at one guy."

"Who's that?" Thomas asked.

On the sideline, Beckenbauer waved to them. "Thomas!" he shouted and beckoned him to come over.

Mats looked at Thomas and smiled. "I think it's you."

Thomas was surprised and did not move for a few seconds. Then he took in a deep breath and trotted over to where Beckenbauer, Stöber, and Kögl were waiting for him.

"Thomas I'd like you to meet..." Beckenbauer never finished his sentence.

Thomas thrust out his hand and shook Stöber's hand. "Mr. Stöber." Then he shook Kögl's hand. "And Mr. Kögl. Very happy to meet you both," he said and flashed them a smile.

Stöber and Kögl looked at each other, then back to Thomas. "You know who we are?" Stöber asked.

Thomas grinned. "Of course. I read *Kicker*."

The men chuckled, surprised at his confidence.

"Thomas is not only a great player here; he's also a great student of the game," Beckenbauer said.

Thomas shrugged. "I love history. Especially when it's about soccer. My grandfather – I never met him because he died before I was born – loved Bayern more than anything. His last wish was to watch a Bayern match on TV."

"What a lovely story," Stöber said. "Did he get his wish?"

Thomas bit his lip, then smiled. "Yes."

The men were clearly moved by Thomas's story.

"Learning everything about the game keeps me connected to him," he said.

Stöber and Kögl turned to Beckenbauer. "Can we talk?" they asked in unison and laughed that they said it together. Beckenbauer knew exactly what they wanted.

He turned to Thomas. "It's six o'clock, time for you to head home," he said.

"Yes, sir," Thomas said and turned to the men. "Nice meeting you." He trotted off toward the changing room.

The train ride home was bumpy and so was the countryside. Short smooth hills with lakes and villages in between, green pastures and fancy train stations passed by between Munich and Tutzing. When he finished his last math problem, he looked up and saw the familiar scenery of the Tutzing station as the suburban whined and slowed to a stop.

His grandmother was on the platform waiting for him, just like always. He gathered up his kit and school things, raced up the aisle, and got out onto the platform. Then he walked to her car. On the short drive home, they talked about his day. Thomas was amazed that she was always interested in his day, even though most of them were exactly the same as the day before. He played well. He had fun. And he finished his homework.

Later that night, he received a phone call. He was offered a place on the U16 national team. It would be his first time playing for Germany.

He was so happy he cried, "Yessss!" after he hung up.

When Thomas was fifteen, Bernd Stöber recruited him to the Under-16 German national team and his first appearance was in Lohne against Russia. Lohne was a seven-hour drive from Munich. Thomas had never been that far away from home in his life. And all he did after that long journey was sit on the bench. Then, in the 70th minute, he went in for Kevin Pezzoni. Stöber thought he played brilliantly.

It was a few weeks later and Thomas's high school teacher stood at the front of the class as the students filed in. "Thomas Muller," she said loudly with her usual authority.

Thomas froze when he came in the door.

"Please come here," she said, cricking her finger at him.

He marched up the aisle and stopped in front of her desk while the rest of the class took their seats.

"Why were you absent yesterday?" she asked.

"Oh! Very sorry. I have a note!" He fished around in his jacket and handed her a folded note.

She unfolded it and read it, then looked up at him, amazed.

"This is from the coach of the DFB?" she sputtered. DFB was the acronym for the German Football Association.

Thomas shrugged. "Yes, ma'am, I play for the U16 squad. Are you a soccer fan?"

All she could do was nod, and wave him off back to his seat, still staring at the note, incredulous.

Thomas smiled, then walked slowly back down the aisle and took his seat.

The teacher looked up and waved the note. "May I keep this?"

Thomas smiled politely and nodded.

That was how it went for Thomas now that he played for the Under-16 national squad. Soccer consumed him as he rose in the ranks. And then, in 2006, when he was 17, he met a girl who had absolutely no interest in soccer.

And his whole life changed.

He went to a high school dance and there she was, across the floor talking to one of his friends. She was tall and beautiful, and he could not believe he had never noticed her before. At that moment, she turned his way and smiled right at him. His friend introduced them. "Lisa Trede," she said and put out her hand. He took it. "Thomas Muller," he said. "Soccer legend."

Lisa smiled. "Never heard of you."

He studied her for a moment, then burst out laughing.

After the dance, they stayed in touch on social media. He discovered she loved horses and so, slowly, he acquired a love for horses as well. She was not much into soccer and left it that way. At least for a while. They were inseparable from the moment they met.

CHAPTER 13
HOPES AND DISAPPOINTMENTS

The Mullers took their places on the family couch in the living room. The television set was tuned to the 2006 World Cup opening game. Germany was the host country and almost everyone believed that the home advantage would play as big a role as it often does. The general mood was confident and joyous. Germany is a soccer-loving country and winning the World Cup on their home turf would be amazing.

The TV sound blasted. The first match, Germany versus Costa Rica, was about to begin in Bayern's home stadium, the Allianz Arena in Munich.

Thomas was grilling the meat on the barbecue, but his eyes were on Lisa, who stood nearby, watching. When he wasn't looking, smoke billowed up from the burning meat.

"Hey! Don't burn it!" Simon said, hurrying out of the house with another tray for the barbecue. He was just fourteen but almost as tall as his older brother. Thomas considered himself an expert on the BBQ.

"Don't worry little brother," he chuckled and flipped the meat.

On TV, the match started.

Thomas rubbed his hands together. "Klinsmann looks confident," he said. "He was a great player. I got a feeling this is his time."

"He looks worried," Klaudia remarked.

"Stop," Gerhard said. "Don't jinx it."

Everyone laughed.

"Watch Lahm. He's going to score," Thomas said, sitting on the edge of his seat on the couch.

"Lahm never scores," his father replied.

But, six minutes into play, midfielder Tim Borowski received the ball and nudged it to the left where left-back Philipp Lahm, picked it up and moved forward. Just outside the eighteen, he fooled Costa Rican keeper Jose Porras, and planted the ball in the net!

"GOOOOAAAALLLLL!!!"

Everyone leaped to their feet, almost tipping the couch over backward. Thomas danced around the room as if he had scored the goal himself.

Germany was up one to zero.

Gerhard looked at his son, incredulous. "Good call."

Thomas grinned. "Thomas Muller. Soccer legend. And clairvoyant. So be careful, I know what you're thinking."

Everyone laughed.

Six minutes later, Costa Rican Paulo Wanchope scored his first, tying the score. But, five minutes after, that Miroslav Klose scored in the 17th minute, and clinched his second in the 61st minute. Wanchope scored for Costa Rica in the 73rd minute, but Frings answered in the 87th minute to seal the score.

Germany won, four to two, and the feast at the Muller house continued until late.

When Thomas came home one day later in the week, Gerhard reached into his back pocket and took out an envelope. "We got this in the mail today," he said, handing it to him. "It was addressed to your mother, but it is for you. A letter from Horst Hrubesch. You know who I'm talking about?"

Thomas nodded quickly and opened the letter. "Of course! The A-Junior trainer."

Gerhard smiled and put his arm over his son's shoulders. "Your mother and I want to be the first to congratulate you, son. Germany wants you for the national U19 squad. Thomas Kraft and Toni Kroos are also going."

Thomas was unsure about the good news. He had already moved up at Bayern under Kurt Niedermayer, but to be moved up nationally was a great surprise.

He looked at his father. It was a great step for him. Maybe, in four years, he would make the next big move and play for the national team. All the pieces were falling into place. And all he wanted now was for Germany to win the World Cup.

Five days later, at FIFA WM-Stadion Dortmund, Germany battled against Poland for ninety long, grueling minutes in front of 65,000 cheering fans and millions of people watching on television sets around the world. Finally, Swiss-born striker Oliver Neuville scored one minute into overtime, giving Germany the win, one to zero. It was a reminder that, in soccer, you can't underestimate your opponent even if it's a lesser team. Nonetheless, it was a win.

Six days after that, toward the end of June, Germany played Ecuador in Berlin and won three to zero. Miroslav Klose got two goals and Podolski scored one. Klose was on a streak to become one of the world's most accomplished strikers. He had a unique ability that he shared with Gerd Muller to finish attacks and find the net time after time. Thomas watched every match, sometimes with Lisa. Winning all their matches in Group A had been expected, but now they'd moved on to the knockout stage, every game was a must-win.

On match days or nights, the taverns in Pähl were full to the brim and spectators spilled out into the main street. The village was giddy with the prospects of a World Cup win for Germany. Their first game in the knockout stage was against Sweden in Munich.

Thomas and Lisa stood in the street outside the tavern and watched the match on a large screen the owners had set up outside their establishment so anyone could watch. And when Podolski scored in the fourth minute, the street erupted in cheering.

Thomas jumped up and down, and so did Lisa. "This is so great!" she said. She was starting to feel it. It was infectious.

Thomas looked at her. "It's the best game in the world. And when our team is winning, it's so amazing!"

Everyone in the tavern and all the people on the street cheered wildly. Podolski had just scored Germany's second goal, and it was only twelve minutes into the match. The score stood until the last minute and Germany moved on to the quarter-finals.

72,000 fans filled the stands, and every television set in Germany was tuned to the World Cup as Germany battled Argentina in the quarter-finals. The first half ended with no goals, and the country was glued to their TV sets, edgy but hopeful. In the 49th minute, Argentina center-back Roberto Ayala scored. There was a collective cry of disappointment. It was the first time Germany had fallen behind in a match since the start of the World Cup.

Thomas sat on the edge of his seat, trying to remain calm.

After thirty more scoreless minutes, Miroslav Klose zeroed-in and equalized the score with a goal in the 80th minute. Again, Klose had come to the rescue when so many eyes had been looking nervously at the clock with time ticking and the game slipping away. The game ended with a tie and went into overtime, but neither team could find the net. When the referee whistled, it was time for the cruel penalty shootout which would send one of the teams home, regardless of their quality.

Thomas groaned. "Oh no! Argentina has never lost a penalty shootout!" It was hard to watch. And he knew how hard it was on the players.

Gerhard put his hand on his son's shoulder. "Neither has Germany," he said.

Neuville went first for Germany. Score!

Next went Cruz for Argentina and made it one to one.

Michael Ballack went next and scored easily. Ayala who'd scored the goal for Argentina in normal time went next and missed!

Podolski went next for Germany and scored! Then Rodriguez scored for Argentina.

Borowski stepped up and, with his sleight of foot, fooled the keeper and scored!

Cambiasso failed when keeper Lehmann blocked the shot. Germany moved on to the semi-finals. What a relief that was! The entire country took a deep breath. The same thought crossed many people's minds: two more games and we have it!

Four long days. Thomas tried to keep his mind off the tournament. Germany was so close. And on the 4th of July, Germany faced off against the great Italian squad in Dortmund.

There were no goals in the first 90 minutes and the match went again into overtime. Then in the 119th minute, when everyone was sure that the game would go into penalties again, Grosso scored for Italy. One more minute left.

In soccer, a lot can be done in one minute. So many games were decided in the very last second of overtime.

But not this time.

Two minutes later, Alessandro Del Piero scored for Italy in the 120+1st minute and that was the end of Germany's run in the World Cup.

Germany was out. They would not be moving on to Berlin for the final.

Thomas was devastated.

He went for a walk down to his grandmother's farm, alone, and leaned against the fence where some cows had congregated. He felt a deep pain.

Erna saw him from her kitchen window and came out of the farmhouse and walked over to him. "Yes, I know. It's the end of the world," she said and put her arm around him. "But what are you going to do about it?"

"I don't know, Grandma," Thomas whispered, wiping his tears away.

"What have I always taught you?"

He looked at her. "Never give up."

She smiled. "You will always succeed. As long as you don't give up." She studied him for a few moments. Thomas said nothing. "What are you thinking?"

Thomas managed a smile. "I'm thinking, someday, I'm going to win this for Germany. I have to."

Erna smiled and hugged him. "That's my boy," she said. "Let's go back, I'll make you some rissoles. Are you hungry?"

They started walking back to her farmhouse. "Starved," he said.

CHAPTER 14
GOOD NEWS

"Muller!" U19 national team coach Horst Hrubesch shouted.

Thomas sat on the bench, watching the match. He was lonely for his family and for Lisa, who was 300 miles away on her farm.

The crowd cheered, and he looked up just in time as his fellow striker, Savio Nsereko, scored a goal, putting his team ahead. When he heard his name, he leaped to his feet. He'd known he would be called, he just didn't know when. Eighty minutes of the international friendly against England had already passed, and he worried he might not go in at all. This was to be his debut for the U19 squad. But his worries were over. Germany was up one-zero and Coach Hrubesch was subbing out Nsereko, the goal scorer, with Thomas.

Nsereko trotted off the Waldstadion Kaiserlinde pitch to the 4,000 cheering fans and high-fived Thomas. Thomas crossed the line to join his Bayern teammates Kevin Pezzoni and Holger Badstuber. His folks, grandmother, and brother were in attendance.

Hrubesch was fifty-six years old and rugged-looking with bleached blond hair. He had a good record as a coach. He turned back and nodded to team manager Frank Kramer. They had told Thomas a day earlier that he would debut, and Thomas had barely slept a wink that night.

Thomas played well. When the full-time whistle blew, he trotted off the field, and a reporter stuck a microphone in his face. That had never happened before. "Muller! How do you think you did?" the reporter asked.

"Magnificently," Thomas replied, with a flourish. When the reporter gave him a surprised look, he added, "At least that's what my mother says!" With that, he continued jogging off the pitch with the rest of his squad, leaving the reporter behind, chuckling.

Thomas felt good about his debut. Although he hadn't scored, he'd worked hard and Germany had left the field victorious. It was November 14th, 2007, and he had just turned 18.

That night, while all the other boys went out to celebrate, Thomas stayed in and studied for his *Arbitur.*

Back at Bayern, he played twenty-four out of twenty-six matches. At the end of the season, he tied with teammate Steffen Schneider with six goals. His pal Toni Kroos had scored seven and was named the highest scorer of the team.

By mid-2008, Thomas had not only finished a successful season in the FC Bayern Youth Program and a great run with the German national U-19 team but he had also finished high school.

A month later, Thomas stood in the middle of his kitchen, staring at another letter. It had come in the mail just minutes before. This one wasn't a letter from another soccer team trying to lure him away. It was from his high school. He ripped it open and began reading. After a few seconds, he smiled broadly. "Oh my God," he muttered.

"What is it?" his mother asked.

"My *Arbitur*," he muttered, without taking his eyes off the letter. He looked up. "I passed."

Klaudia got to her feet and stretched out her arms and engulfed him. "Oh, I am so proud of you!"

Thomas was proud of himself. He had set himself a number of goals, going all the way back to when he was a boy, but graduation had always right on top.

The next week, Hermann Gerland, the trainer of FC Bayern Amateurs II was waiting for him when he left the field on the last day of the season. "We have to talk," Gerland said.

"Uh-oh," Thomas muttered.

Gerland laughed. "What do you mean, 'uh-oh'? Is something wrong?"

"I was going to ask you the same thing," Thomas said. "Whenever someone says 'We have to talk', it usually means I'm in trouble."

Gerland laughed. "Well, we do have to talk. We have to talk about next year. Unless, of course, you have decided to retire from soccer?"

"Not before the World Cup!" Thomas exclaimed.

"Good. Here's a little rule in life for you. When you do something right, you don't get punished," Gerland said.

Thomas wasn't paying attention. He was looking at the trainer's hair.

"What's wrong?"

"You have gray hair," he replied.

"And I earned every one of them," Gerland replied. "Why?"

"I was just hoping they weren't because of me."

Gerland chuckled. "Not all of them," he said. "Listen, the reason I'm here is because I want to give you a shot on the reserve team. And they said yes."

"Bayern II?!" Thomas chimed in.

Gerland shrugged. "Don't get too excited. It's the third division. We finished 8th this season, so we need all the help we can get. But there's more to it than that. I want to get you playing at this level to see if we can move you up to the first team."

Thomas sucked in a breath with surprise.

"What do you think?" Gerland asked.

"I think I'm ready," Thomas replied.

A month later, in March, Thomas was at Bayern II, playing with his teammates to qualify for the new 3rd league that was about to be established.

CHAPTER 15
HEROES

The boys from SpVgg Unterhaching were on him the second he stepped on the field replacing Stephan Furstner in the 72nd minute, but he was faster than all of them.

The Unterhaching defenders tried to catch him. They tried really hard. But they couldn't keep up. He zigged and zagged and was keeping their defense busy and, at a certain moment, he found a gap near the box and waited for the ball he knew would be there a nanosecond later. It was handed to him on a plate and he flicked it into the net in the 88th minute.

Everyone was on their feet as he ran out of the box, arms in the air, and skidded on his knees.

Hermann smiled. And the man that stood by him, the assistant coach, also smiled.

It was Gerd Muller. Thomas's hero. His arms were crossed over his chest. The legendary *Bomber* himself. At that moment on the field, Thomas remembered the time all those years ago when he'd ran after him across the parking lot and caught him at his car and got his autograph. He still had it. It was one of his most cherished possessions. And then there were all the times he had watched him coach the older squads. He had the same smile that was on his poster on the wall in Thomas's bedroom.

Thomas couldn't help himself. So, he waved.

Muller grinned and waved back, then turned to Gerland. "He has it in him, Gerland," he said.

"I know," Gerland nodded.

Thomas's goal was not enough to get a win. They lost two to four, and the team fell to 11th place. But Muller had other ideas for his players. As the squad left the field, he waved Thomas over.

"Y-yes, sir?" Thomas stammered. He was so nervous.

"We need you to play up front more because you are a natural poacher. You'll score more goals!" Gerd said.

Thomas was speechless. The king of poachers was telling him he was a natural goal scorer. Nothing can be better than that.

Gerd smiled. He was used to this. He knew how to handle the fans and he knew how to handle the players. He took one look at Thomas and snapped his fingers in recognition. "I remember you. Parking lot at Bayern after a match. You ran all the way over to me. I signed an autograph card for you." He looked Thomas over. "You grew up," he quipped.

"Y-yes, sir," Thomas said.

Gerd shook his hand. "And now you're on my team!" he said.

Thomas realized the same thing.

"Life has all kinds of twists and turns, doesn't it, Muller?" Gerd asked.

"Y-you're going to help me with my game?" Thomas asked.

"My job is to get you ready for the first team," Gerd said simply.

And, true to his word, in July 2008, Gerd Muller and Hermann Gerland handed their star striker over to Jurgen Klinsmann, the new coach of FC Bayern.

CHAPTER 16

THOMAS'S PREMIERE

Hermann Gerland stood next to Jurgen Klinsmann as he studied the tall boy standing stock-still before them. "Eighteen goals in twenty-six matches is impressive, Muller," Klinsmann said as he walked slowly around the young player, examining him. "I believe that may be a record score in the A-Jugend. No wonder you were champions."

"I guess so," Thomas said.

Klinsmann pointed to Thomas's skinny legs. "And to think you did it all on those stork legs."

Gerland stifled a laugh.

Thomas smiled at Klinsmann. So that was how it was going to be. "Yes sir, but if I may throw in," he began. "I'd say my legs are more like a flamingo's," he quipped, then looked to Gerland for approval.

Gerland rolled his eyes. *Here we go*, he thought.

Everyone laughed. Klinsmann raised an eyebrow at Thomas and when Thomas looked awkward, he turned his back on the boy and smiled. "I believe you are right, Muller," Klinsmann said. "You *are* more like a flamingo. But if *I* may throw in, all of us birds on this squad want you to think of yourself more as... as an *eagle*."

Thomas grinned. "So, you are saying we're all definitely for the birds," he quipped.

Klinsmann and Gerland burst out laughing. "You defy the laws of physics, Muller," Klinsmann said.

"I'll take that as a compliment, sir," Thomas replied.

Thomas finally got to put his previous two weeks of training into action on the field at Waldschlösschen Stadium in Lippstadt for a sold-out friendly match against SV Lippstadt 08. The noise from the crowd was loud and rambunctious.

Thomas lined up with his teammates in the tunnel, out of sight of the crowd. Klinsmann wanted a dramatic entrance.

"That's a lot of noise for 4,000 fans," Michael Rensing said. He was nervous. It was his first time starting as the number one keeper for Bayern.

"That's because that's not 4,000 fans out there. It's 8,000," Thomas said. "I heard it on the radio. Waldschlösschen is bursting at the seams!"

His teammates chuckled.

The match was supposed to start at 4:00 sharp and it was already 3:53 and only the Lippstadt squad had entered the field.

The crowd shouted, *"KLINSMANN! KLINSMANN!"*

Back in the tunnel, Klinsmann stepped up to Rensing. "Ready?"

Rensing nodded.

"Okay," Klinsmann said, and Rensing took the field, followed by Walter Junghans, the goalkeeping coach.

The crowd went crazy as the first of the Bayern team took the field.

In a heartbeat, there was a mob of cameramen snapping pictures of Klinsmann and his squad, blinding them in the dark tunnel.

The loudspeakers came to life. "And now, the coach of Bayern Munich, Jurgen…"

And the crowd answered in unison, "KLINNSSSSMANNNN!"

Klinsmann looked at his men. He didn't have Klose or Schweinsteiger or Lahm or Podolski – they were all out with injuries or still on vacation. But it felt good coming back to the Bundesliga as a coach after the World Cup disappointment. "Let's do this!" he shouted to his team and charged off, followed by the rest, into the light at the end of the tunnel and onto the field.

For a brief moment, Thomas thought it felt like magic. The energy from the crowd was electric.

His teammates wished him luck, and he felt like he belonged. This was his team. All the time growing up, he could not remember a time when someone didn't want him on their team – playing at the High Castle of Pähl, on the school grounds, the basement, and even on the roadway out in front of his grandmother's farm. But this was it. He couldn't ask for more. He stood alongside the other new guy, Joseph Ngwenya from Zimbabwe. And then, in a heartbeat, it was time to go. He bumped fists with Ngwenya.

The new Bayern lineup filed out onto the lush green field of Lippstadt. Rensing, Lell, Breno, van Buyten, Ze Roberto, then van Bommel, Ottl, Sosa, Kroos, and finally Muller and Ngwenya. Defensive midfielder Mark van Bommel was twelve years older than most of the boys and would soon become Bayern's first non-German captain.

The stands were filled with Bayern fans and they were all on their feet, waving and cheering wildly, many of them wearing the Bayern home jersey.

The game started at 4:00 sharp and two minutes and fifty-six seconds later, van Bommel passed to Ze Roberto who sent the ball up to the left of center for Muller, who dusted it into the net, scoring his first goal. And the first goal for the new team manager, Jurgen Klinsmann.

Klinsmann had hoped for the best considering most of his great players were not there, but he hadn't expected the greatness that was delivered that afternoon in Lippstadt. Bayern won seven to one.

Muller scored a hat-trick. Klinsmann was impressed.

After the triumphant match, the team showered and dressed, then filed onto the team bus. When Thomas boarded, Hermann Gerland was there to announce his arrival. "Attention, gentlemen," he shouted through a bullhorn, standing at the front of the team bus. "Radio Pähl is on the air again!"

At that exact moment, Thomas came bounding up the metal stairs and seemed to blow onto the bus like a hurricane. Everyone on the bus cheered and applauded. They expected a performance and Thomas was always good for one.

"Thank you, thank you," Thomas said, bowing to his audience. "Really, you are too kind."

Klinsmann, in the front seat on the bus, leaned against the bulkhead and shook his head in amusement.

"Hey, Thomas, when we get back to Munich, which end of the bus should we get off on?" Toni Kroos shouted at him from the back of the bus.

"It doesn't matter!" Thomas shouted back. "Both ends stop!"

Everyone laughed, including the driver, who started the engine and lurched the bus onto the highway and headed for home. Thomas made his way down the aisle, grabbed the seat next to Kroos, and high-fived him. "Thanks for the set-up – on and off-field!"

"Any time," Kroos said. He liked playing Thomas's straight man, on and off the field. He plugged in his earbuds and stretched out his legs. It was a long ride back to Munich.

CHAPTER 17
THE SHOWDOWN

Lisa lit a fire in the big stone fireplace at her parent's home and hid the book she was reading when Thomas came in carrying a tray of coffees. She had scattered a few large throw pillows on the floor in front of the roaring hearth and leaned against the one with the book hidden underneath. Thomas didn't know it, but she had a trick up her sleeve. He was always playing practical jokes on her. Now it was her turn.

Thomas came over and sat beside her, leaning on a nearby pillow. She took his hands in hers. "I have something to tell you," she said.

Thomas blushed. Was this another one of those signals that meant something bad was coming? He hoped she didn't notice he was nervous.

"Y-you want to tell me something?" Thomas stammered.

Lisa smiled at his discomfort. "Yes, why? Does that make you nervous?"

Thomas shook his head, a little too quickly Lisa thought. "Relax. It's about soccer," she said.

"Soccer? You want to tell me something about soccer?"

"As a matter of fact, I am quite interested in your beautiful game," she said. "What I wanted to tell you was that I've been getting more into it lately. Especially the practices and tactics."

"Practices and tactics?" He laughed, then wished he hadn't. He didn't want to hurt her feelings. "What do you know about practices and tactics?"

Lisa frowned. "I know plenty, smarty," she said, pretending to be mad.

"Oh really? What's your favorite?" He was half-serious. He figured she would not have an answer.

"The Libero Tactic," she said boldly without hesitation.

Thomas was surprised she'd named one. Then, he thought about it and burst out laughing.

She was shocked at his reaction. "Why are you laughing?"

"That tactic hasn't been used in twenty years!" he said.

Lisa bit her lip to keep from laughing herself. "You are so mean!" She dove on him, tackling him. "Take it back! Take it back!" she shouted and pinned him to the stone floor.

"Okay, okay, I take it back!" Thomas laughed, and she let him go.

Thomas grinned. "If you're really interested, how about I show you something a little more... current?" he said. "Like watching me play?"

She laughed. He loved to make her laugh.

Two weeks later, while he suffered in silence, Thomas closed his eyes and thought about that moment. He was on the bench and was upset because Klinsmann hadn't included him in his opening lineup. Thomas thought he deserved it and was itching to make his Bundesliga debut. It was August 15th, and they were playing Hamburger SV. In the 79th minute, Klinsmann told him, "You're in for Klose."

Thomas got up and stomped his feet while Klinsmann watched with amusement. "Something wrong with your feet?" he asked.

"They fell asleep," Thomas replied and headed for the sideline just as Miroslav Klose trotted off. Thomas scored after his first two minutes on the field. But that didn't seem to matter to Klinsmann.

Thomas played three more times in the season, in games against Arminia Bielefeld, Borussia Mönchengladbach, and finally Energie Cottbus. He didn't score in any of those games and spent the rest of the season in the 3rd league with the second team where he scored fifteen goals in thirty-two matches. He had a lot of fun, but it wasn't the real deal.

A few weeks later, after practice, he was invited into Hermann Gerland's office. Klinsmann was already there.

"I want to sell you to a team where you will be able to play more," Klinsmann told him.

"But I like playing for Bayern," Thomas said. "I just need to play more. I'll show you what I'm worth."

"I understand Thomas, but I have a roster I am happy with and there's just no room for you on the first team."

Hermann sat silently on the corner of his desk.

Klinsmann's words stung.

"Give me a chance, Coach," Thomas said.

"Hoffenheim needs a versatile attacker like you," Klinsmann said. "They have been trying to lure you away from us for months. I think you will be very happy there."

Thomas was devastated.

"Why don't you step out?" Hermann finally spoke up. "I want to speak with Coach Klinsmann alone."

"Yes, sir," Thomas said and left the room. But he stayed in the hall outside the room and listened to them talk.

"Thomas is happy here, Jurgen," Gerland told Klinsmann. "He grew up here. He belongs with us. With Bayern."

"But his technical skills are just not there yet," Klinsmann said.

"This kid always achieved his goals. Our goals. He has a lot to give us."

Klinsmann sighed. "I think we ought to give him a shot with another team, don't you, Hermann?"

"No Jurgen, I don't. And I strongly advise you to get the idea out of your head."

Klinsmann was taken aback by his insistence. He stood up and gathered his papers into a folder. "We'll talk again," he said and started to leave the office. Out in the hallway, Thomas spun around and walked away as Klinsmann exited the office.

"Not on my watch," Gerland said to himself and glanced outside and saw Thomas.

"Besides," Hermann shouted after Klinsmann. "The trade window is closed." Klinsmann ignored him and kept walking. Hermann turned to Thomas. "Sorry you had to hear that." He went back into the office.

"Thanks, Coach," Thomas said, mostly to himself. He leaned against the wall, relieved.

A few weeks later, Jurgen Klinsmann was fired, and the sale of Thomas Muller never happened.

There was one more major event that month. Thomas asked Lisa to marry him.

And Lisa said *yes*.

CHAPTER 18

THE SMILING CHAMPION

"With me, Muller will always play," Louis van Gaal said into the tangled jungle of microphones in front of him, surrounded in front by a gaggle of animated reporters. Thomas Muller, Holger Badstuber, and Basti Schweinsteiger were behind him. "This is my dream team!" he continued.

Van Gaal, a Dutchman, had just taken the helm of the Bayern first team, replacing Jurgen Klinsmann. The press conference was just the start. There was a season to play. He didn't mind speaking his mind to the press; he got along with them just fine, and this was news. He wanted to win all the titles, which was expected of him. And when Thomas let him know he was willing to play anywhere as long as he was played, Van Gaal said, "Oh, don't worry about that, I meant what I said. You will play."

"Where?" Thomas asked.

"We'll figure it out," Van Gaal replied. He knew that with Thomas he had a relentless player who could create havoc in the box, score goals from close range, and always find another striker open for a killer pass. Thomas was a false 9 kind of player, and Van Gaal knew he could play him up top, right, left, or in the middle, behind his center-forward and sometimes ahead of him. He was a player that was always on the move and gave everything he had for the entire game.

Thomas's eyes lit up when he thought about that.

Unfortunately, by November, it looked as if Van Gaal's dream team was going to be knocked out of the first-round Champions League.

As Thomas had promised a year earlier when he got engaged to Lisa Trede, he married her on December 1st, 2009. They were wed at the registry office in Ismaning. After the ceremony, they went home to their ranch near Munich.

During the season, Van Gaal kept his word and played Thomas in every match, including the Champions League final against Inter Milan. They lost, but Thomas played brilliantly.

Earlier in the season, in October 2009, a man appeared from the Bayern tunnel and stood in the shadows during practice. When the action stopped, Thomas saw him first as just a silhouette in the shadow of the tunnel, but when he stepped out into the light, Thomas smiled.

It was one of his heroes, Oliver Bierhoff. The manager of the German national team. The man on the other poster on the wall in his boyhood bedroom.

Hermann Gerland went over to Thomas. "He's here to see you," Gerland said.

Thomas hurried over to greet the man who had scored the golden goal that won Germany a trophy in 1996.

Bierhoff crossed his arms and sized Thomas Muller up when he approached. Thomas thrust out his hand and Bierhoff shook it. "Let's walk," Bierhoff said.

"You are doing a great job here in the U-21 and we are considering you for the World Cup squad. Joachim Löw and Gerd Muller and I had a long talk about you. We want you to play with us next month in two international friendlies and we'll go from there."

Thomas couldn't believe it. This was like a dream come true. "I gotta tell you something," Thomas said.

"All right."

"I have you on my wall," he said. "The poster is the one of you making that golden goal."

"You have me on your wall, and we want you on our team," Bierhoff said with a smile.

In March 2010, Thomas was called up to make his debut with the first team. The match was a friendly with Argentina and played on Thomas's home turf at the Allianz Arena. He opened and was subbed in the 67th minute. Argentina won one to zero. Soccer legend Diego Maradona was the Argentina coach. After the match, there was the customary press conference.

Maradona was already seated behind the microphone when Thomas stepped onto the dais, sat down two chairs away from him, and nodded to him respectfully.

"Who is this?" Maradona sneered. "The ball boy?"

He was surely expecting the German coach Löw to step in.

There were uneasy chuckles from the press and the audience.

Thomas was embarrassed. "Thomas Muller, sir." Then added under his breath, "Soccer legend."

Maradona stood up, mortified. "Conference over." He spun on his heel and walked off, leaving Thomas and the others alone at the dais.

"Was it something I said?" Thomas quipped, and everyone laughed.

Thomas was selected to the final roster of the 2010 national lineup for the 2010 World Cup in South Africa. He was handed the number 13 jersey. Michael Ballack's jersey. This was special because it was the jersey number Gerd Muller had worn in 1974 when he shot the victory goal in the World Cup final against the Netherlands. And the jersey Thomas had worn almost every day to school as a boy – when it was clean. He took it and pulled it on. He was moved to tears. It meant the world to him.

"Michael is out with injuries and won't be able to make the World Cup this year," Löw said. "It's yours!"

Thomas joined the likes of Bastian Schweinsteiger Manuel Neuer, Lukas Podolski, Mario Gómez, Miroslav Klose, Philipp Lahm, Jérôme Boateng, Badstuber, Mesut Özil, and Sammy Khedira. It was the youngest German squad in 75 years, with Joachim Löw in charge.

Germany played their first match for Group D on June 13th, three days into the tournament, against Australia in Durban. Podolski scored in the 8th minute, Klose in the 26th, Muller in the 68th, and Cacau in the 70th. Thomas's first goal in the World Cup. He was thrilled, but he knew it was only the beginning.

In their third appearance in the group stage against Ghana at Soccer City in Johannesburg, Özil struck their only goal in the 60th minute. Germany won one to zero and Özil was named *Man of the Match*. Thomas fought hard and shined in the round of sixteen against England where he scored his second World Cup goal and was selected *Man of the Match*. Germany beat England four to one and ensured they moved on to the quarter-finals against Argentina in Cape Town.

Three minutes into the quarter-final match against a formidable Argentina lineup that included Barcelona star Leo Messi, Argentinian coach Maradona was livid. He had barely warmed his seat when Germany scored a goal.

"Who scored?" Maradona asked his assistant coach.

"Muller," replied his assistant.

"The skinny one?" Maradona wondered. He thought he'd seen the tall, lanky player once, but he couldn't remember where or when.

After the goal celebration, Thomas's eyes met Maradona's. He knew the *Hand of God* would never call him a ball boy again.

Thomas's goal was just the opener. Germany thrashed Maradona's team, four to zero, with two more goals by Klose and one by Friedrich, and sent humiliated Argentina home.

But the German machine was stopped by Spain on July 7th, when Germany lost zero to one. They wouldn't be bringing the trophy home to Germany.

The team was overwhelmed. The German dream was crushed, although the Löw vision of a new young and energetic team was starting to take shape. The style of play, the talent, the team effort was all on display in South Africa. The future was shaping up, and it was promising.

In the game for third place with Uruguay, Thomas made his mark early with his fifth goal in South Africa. He had already had one effort ruled out for offside when he fired Löw's side ahead in the 19th minute. Germany won three to two and Thomas was named *Man of the Match*.

Thomas won the Golden Boot, scoring five goals in his first World Cup.

After the game, he went to the locker room holding something behind his back.

"What's that you got behind you?" Manuel Neuer asked with a smile. He already knew.

Thomas revealed what he was hiding: a bright red bullhorn.

"Oh no," Podolski said, knowing what was coming next.

Thomas put the bullhorn to his lips and pulled the trigger. "Give me an H!"

There was laughter all around as they all chimed in. "H!" They knew where he was going.

"Give me a U!" Thomas shouted, and his teammates answered. "Give me an M!" Thomas said, then, "Give me a B!"

"B!" The German national team were all on their feet now, shouting back, their voices echoing off the walls of the changing room.

"Give me an A!" Thomas yelled and his friends yelled back.

Then they all started singing in unison, *Humba Humba Humba Tät*erä Täterä Täterä.

It was a carnival song the Bayern teams sang to get themselves in a winning mood. They were still singing when Löw and Bierhoff came in, so the bosses joined in, arm-in-arm with their team, their voices echoing off the walls and all the way out to the field. The German national team may have come third, but they were first in song.

And spirit.

CHAPTER 19
THE SPACE INVESTIGATOR

Thomas stepped off the jet from Frankfurt and was hit with a blast of hot, steamy air. "Whoa!" he shouted to his teammates over the cacophony of jets taking off and landing. The Rio de Janeiro/Galeão Antonio Carlos Jobim International Airport was one of the busiest in the world and Jobim's music was playing everywhere. The terminal debarkation tunnel was sealed in canvas but offered little insulation from the oppressive Brazilian heat. It was Thomas's first time on the continent of South America and he was already sweating.

His teammates laughed and urged him to hurry forward. They'd been on the plane for over ten hours and wanted off. The German national squad was down below the equator in the Southern Hemisphere in anticipation of the 2014 World Cup, which would start on the 12th of June and there was a lot of work to do before they took the field for the first game against Portugal at the *Itaipava Arena Fonte Nova Salvador* four days later.

The team had four days to prepare for their start, but Thomas had had four years. The German loss in 2010 had hardened his resolve to win. There had also been a disappointing show in the Euros in 2012, but he matured as a player as did most of his teammates and Löw's vision was coming together. He had already scored eight goals in the World Cup qualifiers leading up to Brazil and he wasn't going to let up on the momentum.

His desire to achieve paid off in Germany's first group game against Portugal. Twelve minutes in, he converted a penalty and scored his first goal of the 2014 World Cup finals. He would score two more in the game, making it a hat-trick, and Germany destroyed Portugal four to zero.

Five days later, they played Ghana to a two to two draw in Fortaleza, with all the goals coming in the second half. Thomas, frustrated, scored no goals. As it turned out, Ghana was the only team Germany could not beat this time. They beat the USA one to zero, and Thomas was voted *Man of the Match* after scoring their only goal in the 55th minute. From there, Germany moved to the round of sixteen where they beat Algeria two to one in extra time with Özil putting them ahead in the 119th minute. In the quarter-final game against France, Thomas's friend Mats Hummels scored the only goal and Germany won one to zero.

The game against Brazil in the semi-finals was one of the most memorable games in the history of the World Cup. Germany defeated the host team in a way that was surprising and humiliating while the entire world watched in disbelief. Thomas scored first in the 11th minute. Then came Klose, then Kroos with two more goals, then Khedira, and finally Schurrle closed the deal with two more goals in the 69th and 79th minutes. With a stunning seven to one win over Brazil, Germany was on the threshold of the final.

Once more, Thomas was going to face Leo Messi and company in a World Cup showdown, this time in a final. He already had five goals but without winning the biggest trophy of all, his personal accomplishments and what the team had done so far didn't matter to him.

They had to win this time.

It was about time. And they were ready.

The match was at the Maracanã in Rio on July 13th.

The two teams looked like formidable gladiators. They were well-matched in talent and shape, but nobody seemed to find the net and the game went to overtime with a penalty shootout looming as the clock ran out.

With only seven minutes of the 120 minutes remaining, Schurrle wove his way through three Argentine defenders on the left and flicked the ball to Götze who was in the clear. Götze took the ball on his chest, then rocketed the ball into the far corner of the net. One to zero to Germany!

Seven minutes later, Germany went into the history books.

When asked what Thomas brought to the game, his coaches and managers all agreed he brought his intense passing combined with his intelligence to cut off all the passing angles. Muller was always on the move, finding space, or creating space for his teammates. The way he made runs was perfect for Bayern Munich and Germany because he played with highly technical and intelligent players.

Thomas once gave himself a nickname that stuck. *The Space Investigator.* Many tried to figure out what he meant, and many more wondered just what made Thomas such a unique player.

Thomas always gave the same answer to explain his nickname: "I see shortcuts on the field. I may look like a stork or a flamingo, but I am most definitely an eagle. I am the *Space Investigator.*"

"How do you do it?" a reporter asked him. "What do you look for?"

Thomas smiled. "I look for air. I look for the absence of players. And then I do what I am supposed to do. I score or I pass."

Thomas's dreams had become a reality. Germany was bringing home the trophy for the first time in twenty-four years. He had scored five goals and become only the third player in soccer history to score at least five goals in each of his first two World Cups, after Teofilo Cubillas and his own teammate Miroslav Klose. With ten World Cup goals, he tied with Helmut Rahn.

But the greatest thing of all was that his beloved Germany had won.

They were world champions for the fourth time.

And this time, when Thomas stood on the podium with his teammates and they hoisted the championship trophy high, and Thomas flashed his championship smile, he became a household name all over the world. He became a national hero.

And Thomas finally knew, in his heart of hearts, that his grandfather was smiling down on him.

CHAPTER 20
THE GREAT COMEBACK

When Thomas turned 30, many believed that his soccer career was over. Failing to win the World Cup in 2018 and the disappointing performance of the national team led Joachim Löw to release Thomas from the team, along with his friends Mats Hummels and Jérôme Boateng, saying he was going for a younger team.

Thomas was surprised and angry.

Funny how things change when you don't win the World Cup, he thought. There was no denying that the national team had failed miserably in the World Cup. But he knew he still had it in him.

Things weren't pretty at Bayern either. Niko Kovač, the team coach, benched Thomas for five games. He made it clear that Thomas wasn't a mainstay in his opening squad anymore.

Lisa watched her husband reading the paper. "What are you thinking?"

Thomas shrugged. "They say my career is over."

She took the paper from him and carefully folded it.

"They are wrong," she said, and he smiled.

"Do I need to change anything?"

"No," she said. "Be yourself."

Thomas got the opportunity to show his worth when Hansi – Hans Dieter Flick, who had joined Bayern Munich on July 1st, 2019 as an assistant coach under Kovač – became the interim coach following a one to five loss to Frankfurt. Kovač was fired and Flick was named interim manager.

When Hansi, who had been assistant coach on the 2014 winning squad, had a private talk with Thomas, he told him, "I have great plans for you. I know you can help us win again."

"I won't disappoint you, Coach," Thomas said and couldn't stop smiling the entire day.

Under Flick, the club won the league, having played the most successful leg of a Bundesliga season in history.

And then they won the Cup.

"I've known Thomas for a long time," Flick told German broadcaster ARD after Bayern's Cup triumph. "He is very important for a coach because he translates the coaching philosophy and tactics onto the field."

The club president said, "Thomas embodies Bayern and represents the club excellently. Every success and title in the last decade are closely tied with the name Thomas Muller. Also, this season Thomas is showing his importance."

Then came the Champions League quarter-finals. The world was reeling when Bayern beat FC

Barcelona eight to two. Thomas scored twice and was all over the pitch, passing brilliantly and working intensely every minute of the game.

Bayern moved on and beat Lyon three to zero in the semi-final. And everyone was talking about Thomas Muller again.

And then came the final. And he showed up to the occasion.

It had to be him, one way or another. Throughout the evenly matched Champions League final, the knobby-kneed figure in the deep forward position roamed everywhere, disrupting the patterns of PSG and teleporting himself into useful attacking spaces. He played soccer with his toes and thighs and elbows in the middle of all that high-speed grace.

Thomas had been at Bayern for 20 years by then. He was an oddly timeless figure, but not a super-athlete. He was, though, a soccer player who knew how to win and understood the movements around him and the way spaces open and close.

Against all odds, he lifted the trophy again.

With a huge smile on his face.

THE WORLDS #1 BEST-SELLING SOCCER SERIES!

THE FLEA

The Amazing Story of Leo
Messi

Michael Part

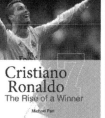

Cristiano Ronaldo
The Rise of a Winner

Michael Part

Neymar
The Wizard

Michael Part

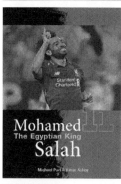

Mohamed
The Egyptian King
Salah

Michael Part & Kevin Ashby

Harry
The Hurricane
Kane

Michael Part

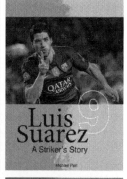

Luis
Suarez
A Striker's Story

Michael Part

James
The Incredible
Number 10

Michael Part

Eden Hazard
The Wonder Boy

Michael Part

Antoine
Griezmann
The Kid Who Never Gave Up

Michael Part & Steve Berg

Made in the USA
Middletown, DE
22 January 2023